SCHOOL SUCCESS FOR AT-RISK STUDENTS

School Success for At-Risk Students: A Culturally Responsive Tiered Approach introduces a model that incorporates cultural responsiveness into the familiar three-tiered model of behavioural and academic support. The model is designed to modify learning environments to support all students, identify students at risk, and provide a continuum of supports for those who need it.

The characteristics, outcomes, and support needs of at-risk students are explored in detail. These students include those with disabilities, those who are English language learners, refugees, indigenous, LGBT+, students from low SES backgrounds, and those who are involved with the juvenile justice or out-of-home care systems. The concepts of cultural responsiveness and competence are defined and discussed, then incorporated into a framework that includes the Response to Intervention and Positive Behavioural Interventions and Supports frameworks. This revised framework is investigated in regards to theory, research, and practice. The importance of cultural competence for at-risk students and ways to improve this in schools are suggested.

This book is a necessary companion for educators and researchers who have an interest in exploring the nature and context of educating at-risk students from the perspective of a culturally responsive multi-tiered system of support. It will also be of interest to a wide range of individuals working in education with at-risk youth, including preservice and veteran teachers, leadership teams, school psychologists, and school counsellors, as well as teacher educators.

Dr Therese M. Cumming is Associate Professor in Special Education at UNSW Australia. Her publications include an edited book (*Sustaining Mobile Learning: Theory, Research, and Practice*, 2016), two co-authored books (*School Connectedness of Students with Disabilities*; *Lifespan Transitions for Individuals with Disabilities: A Holistic Perspective*, 2016), book chapters, journal articles, and international conference papers. She also has many years of experience as a special educator.

Dr Cathi Draper Rodriguez is Professor and Chair of the Department of Education and Leadership. She is a Nationally Certified School Psychologist. She has focused her research on using technology with English learners with and without disabilities, the diagnosis of disabilities in English learners, assessment in education, and multicultural education.

SCHOOL SUCCESS FOR AT-RISK STUDENTS

A Culturally Responsive Tiered Approach

Therese M. Cumming and Cathi Draper Rodriguez

Routledge
Taylor & Francis Group
LONDON AND NEW YORK

First published 2019
by Routledge
2 Park Square, Milton Park, Abingdon, Oxon OX14 4RN

and by Routledge
711 Third Avenue, New York, NY 10017

Routledge is an imprint of the Taylor & Francis Group, an informa business

British Library Cataloguing-in-Publication Data
A catalogue record for this book is available from the British Library

Library of Congress Cataloging-in-Publication Data
Names: Cumming, Therese M., author. | Rodriguez, Cathi Draper, author.
Title: School success for at-risk students : a culturally responsive tiered approach / Therese M. Cumming and Cathi Draper Rodriguez.
Description: Abingdon, Oxon ; New York, NY : Routledge, 2018. | Includes bibliographical references.
Identifiers: LCCN 2018021006 | ISBN 9781138104891 (hbk) | ISBN 9781138104884 (pbk) | ISBN 9781315101996 (ebk)
Subjects: LCSH: Problem youth—Education—United States. | Problem youth—Behavior modification—United States. | Youth with social disabilities—Education—United States.
Classification: LCC LC4802 .C85 2018 | DDC 371.826/94—dc23
LC record available at https://lccn.loc.gov/2018021006

ISBN: 978-1-138-10489-1 (hbk)
ISBN: 978-1-138-10488-4 (pbk)
ISBN: 978-1-315-10199-6 (ebk)

Typeset in Bembo
by Apex CoVantage, LLC

MIX
Paper from responsible sources
FSC™ C013985

Printed in the United Kingdom
by Henry Ling Limited

DEDICATION

TMC – I dedicate this book to my wonderful husband, Jim, my daughter, Emily, and my families – biological, academic, and chosen. Your unending love, support, and laughter inspires me to want to make a difference every day.

CDR – To my husband, Xavier, and two boys, Alex and Zack – You are my everything.

CONTENTS

List of figures and tables *viii*
About the authors *ix*

1 Introduction 1

2 Research and theory framing the multi-tiered culturally responsive system of support model 12

3 At-risk students: English learners, migrant/refugee, and indigenous students 29

4 At-risk students: students with disabilities, mental health issues, and chronic illness 44

5 At-risk students: students in out-of-home care, involvement with the juvenile justice system, and from low SES backgrounds 61

6 At-risk students: LGBT+ 78

7 Developing a culturally competent school climate 92

8 Conclusion 101

Index *104*

FIGURES AND TABLES

Figures

1.1 The PBIS pyramid 4
2.1 Multi-tiered culturally responsive system of support (MTCRSS) 13

Tables

4.1 Comparison of disability reporting categories across countries 46
4.2 DSM-5 diagnostic criteria for ADHD: symptoms of inattention, hyperactivity, and impulsivity 47
5.1 Types of out-of-home care placements 65

ABOUT THE AUTHORS

Therese M. Cumming is Associate Professor in the School of Education at UNSW Australia. She has conducted special education research projects in both the US and Australia. She has authored and co-authored numerous publications, including books, book chapters, and journal articles in the areas of behavioural support, transitions, mobile technology, social skills instruction, and inclusive research. Prior to her university and research work, Therese had 18 years teaching experience in mainstream, special, and mental health settings. Her ongoing research interests come under the umbrella of transition and include the use of technology to support students and families, Positive Behavioural Interventions and Supports, and inclusive education across the lifespan.

Cathi Draper Rodriguez, Ph.D., NCSP, is Professor and Chair in the Education and Leadership Department at Cal State University, Monterey Bay. Dr Draper Rodriguez teaches courses related to assessment, research, and school psychology. Since earning her doctorate from UNLV, she has focused her research on using technology with English learners with and without disabilities, the diagnosis of disabilities in English learners, assessment in education, and multicultural education. Dr Draper Rodriguez is a Nationally Certified School Psychologist. Her previous work experience includes serving as a bilingual school psychologist in a public school setting and as an early interventionist providing services to young Latina mothers.

1

INTRODUCTION

There is an increasing focus on improving the academic and social outcomes of students labelled "at-risk" in today's schools. Students at risk include those with complex needs due to disability, mental illness, behavioural issues, drug and alcohol problems, low socioeconomic status, and family dysfunction (Dowse, Cumming, Strnadová, Lee, & Trofimovs, 2014). The term at-risk can also be applied to students who are English learners, migrants, refugees, indigenous, or non-majority students in their school and/or community (Quinn, Rutherford, Leone, Osher, & Poirer, 2005). Lesbian, gay, bisexual, and transgender (LGBT) students are also an at-risk population, as the bullying and harassment they typically receive at school leads to poor outcomes (GLEN, 2016). At-risk students have historically experienced poorer outcomes throughout their lifespan, such as: poor relationships with peers and adults, low academic achievement, school suspension and expulsion, dropping out of high school, high divorce rates, high rates of substance abuse, and involvement with the justice system. It has been suggested that often there is a disconnect between the students and the school system, causing disengagement (Leone & Mayer, 2004). Gagnon and Richards (2008) suggests that several school factors are responsible, including: (a) poor school climate, (b) classroom setting events, (c) teacher-student communication, (d) high-stakes testing, (e) exclusionary discipline practices, and (f) lack of attention to diversity.

The literature in the field provides a solid evidence base for several academic and behavioural initiatives to improve the outcomes of at-risk students. These tend to be multi-tiered systems of support and are gaining momentum internationally due to their strong evidence base (Sugai & Simonsen, 2012). Two of the most prevalent are Response to Intervention (RtI) and Positive Behavioural Interventions and Supports (PBIS). The focus of the RtI framework is primarily academic, while PBIS is largely centred around improving social and behavioural outcomes. These two frameworks are complementary to one another and, as such, are often seen combined into one framework or multi-tiered systems of support (MTSS) to more seamlessly meet the needs of a diverse population of students (Fuchs & Deshler, 2007). A glaring omission of both of the frameworks and MTSS is that none contain advice on how to implement their evidence-based strategies in a culturally responsive manner to support the diverse range of today's students. The following provides descriptions of RtI, PBIS, MTSS, and cultural responsiveness and introduces a new model that incorporates all three concepts.

Response to Intervention

The Response to Intervention (RtI) approach measures student academic progress against research-based interventions. This model involves educators providing high-quality research-based instructional interventions that match student needs. Student response to the research-based interventions is measured in terms of progress towards achieving outcomes in the academic area. Students who are identified as having difficulties in the general education setting receive specific interventions to remediate the problems. It is only when these research-based interventions do not help the student succeed that the student is referred on for a special education evaluation. The RtI model does not require that a student's cognitive ability be measured against their academic performance, as measured by standardised tests, prior to receiving any sort of special education services.

Response to Intervention models use individualised student assessment that is comprehensive and guides interventions (National Research Center on Learning Disabilities, NRCLD, 2004). The core concepts of RtI include the following (NRCLD, 2004):

1 High-quality instruction in the general education setting.
2 Instruction is research based.
3 Educators assume a role in all students' access to the curriculum.
4 School-wide screening of academics and behaviour.
5 Continuous monitoring of student performance.
6 Use of monitoring to identify student difficulties.
7 Implementation of research-based interventions to meet student need.
8 Assessment of the validity of interventions.
9 Progress monitoring to determine effectiveness of interventions, with changes made as needed.

Response to Intervention is typically presented in a three-tier model, though four- and five-tier models are available. In Tier 1, *primary prevention*, the changes to education occur in the general education setting (O'Connor & Sanchez, 2011). In this tier, schools must ensure that all students in the school have access to a high-quality, research-based general education curriculum. Universal precaution strategies (e.g., universal screening and evidenced-based instruction) are used to ensure that all students can access what is being taught. A substantial amount of research exists to show that poor teaching impacts the amount of academic growth students are able to make. For this reason, another important component of Tier 1 is professional development for teachers and other educators in the setting. This professional development should occur around academics as well as behaviour. If good instruction is being provided to all students in the classroom, the need to provide individualised interventions to students is greatly reduced. This tier is preventive and proactive. During this tier, every student in the school has their academics and behaviour screened. These screenings help to identify students who are in need of intervention, as well as allow the school to measure the effectiveness of the general education curricula. Students who are identified as at-risk during Tier 1 are moved to Tier 2.

In Tier 2, *secondary prevention*, students who are at-risk receive targeted short-term interventions (O'Connor & Sanchez, 2011). Even the most effective classrooms have approximately 20–30% of students who remain at risk for difficulties in reading or in need of other supports (Wanzek & Vaughn, 2007). While in this tier, students receive interventions which are meant to supplement, not supplant, the general education curriculum. Many times, these needs are met through focused interventions. This is often accomplished through small group interventions. Some student study teams use a problem-solving model to identify the appropriate intervention for the student, while others use a list of pre-approved research-based interventions as the way to pick intervention. The students' progress towards a predefined goal is then measured more frequently (monthly or bimonthly). Students who respond to the targeted intervention are placed back into Tier 1. Students who do not respond to their targeted interventions are then referred to Tier 3. Students who return to general education but once again fall behind without the targeted intervention may also be referred to Tier 3.

Tier 3, *tertiary interventions or special education*, of the RtI model includes intensive and individualised intervention. This may also include a referral to Special Education Services. When the interventions being provided in Tier 2 are not sufficient to help the student make the progress that they need, the student then progresses to Tier 3. Tier 3 is different from Tier 2 in that the intervention provided is more precise, focuses on the remediation of skills, and is provided for a longer period of time and occurs in smaller groups (e.g., 1–3 students; Haager, Klinger, & Vaughn, 2007; Harn, Kame'enui, & Simmons, 2007; Vaughn, Linan-Thompson, & Hickman, 2003). In Tier 3 of RtI, the student's progress is monitored more frequently, weekly or biweekly. Through this RtI model, it is thought that the needs of all students will be met more frequently without having to wait for students to fail in order to receive support. These is now research to support the use of RtI to improve the academic skills of students, particularly in the area of literacy, and reduce the number of referrals to special education (Gunn, Biglan, Smolkowski, & Ary, 2000; Shaywitz et al., 2004; Simmons, Kame'enui, Coyne, & Chard, 2002; VanDerHeyden, Witt, & Gilbertson, 2007; Vaughn et al., 2003; Vellutino et al., 1996). Some students have support needs in non-academic areas; Positive Behaviour

Interventions and Supports (PBIS) is a similar model to support students in the area of social, emotional, and behavioural needs.

Positive Behaviour Interventions and Supports (PBIS)

PBIS is a framework of evidence-based practices to enhance social and behavioural outcomes for all students (OSEP Technical Assistance Center on Positive Behavioural Interventions and Supports, 2015). It is most effective when implemented as a school-wide program. PBIS is a three-tiered model aimed at preventing problem behaviour by providing students with a supportive environment. It has seven core features: (a) implementation fidelity, (b) continuum of evidence-based interventions, (c) content expertise and fluency, (d) leadership team implementation and coordination, (e) continuous progress monitoring, (f) universal and comprehensive screening, and most recently (g) cultural and contextual relevance (OSEP Technical Assistance Center on Positive Behavioural Interventions and Supports, 2015). These features are implemented within the tiers, which are depicted in Figure 1.1, and described in detail later.

Tier 1

The first, or primary, tier is known as the universal tier. This tier is focussed on the prevention of problem behaviours through the implementation of high-quality learning environments in all settings – the school, classroom, and other areas, such as hallways, playgrounds, and the lunchroom. All adults in the environment use a common language, common practices, and consistent application of positive and negative reinforcement (OSEP Technical Assistance Center on Positive Behavioural Interventions and Supports, 2017). Tier 1 supports are centred around rules, routines, and quality physical requirements. These are developed by school staff and are positively stated, taught, and modelled. Students are provided with opportunities to practice skills and reinforced when observed behaving appropriately. A continuum of procedures for discouraging problem behaviour are developed, as are procedures for encouraging school-family partnerships.

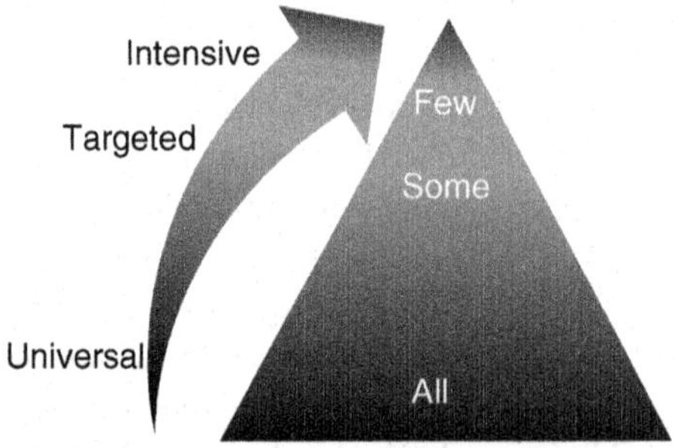

FIGURE 1.1 The PBIS pyramid

When implemented with fidelity, Tier 1 interventions will work with 80% of the school's student population and result in a decrease of office discipline referrals (ODRs) (Horner, Sugai, & Anderson, 2010). ODRs are one way to assess which students need more intensive interventions, as part of the formal process for screening and identifying students in need of more than Tier 1 support. The school's PBIS team may decide that if a student receives a certain amount of ODRs within a certain timeframe, he or she may need to be considered for more intensive Tier 2 interventions.

Tier 2

The secondary, or targeted, tier aims to reduce the prevalence of existing problem behaviours that have been resistant to primary intervention strategies. The practices in this tier are implemented with small groups of ten or fewer students, and are more focused, intensive, and frequent than the universal strategies implemented in Tier 1. Students targeted for Tier 2 interventions will receive increased adult supervision, opportunities for positive reinforcement, and antecedent manipulation such as pre-correction. Interventions in this tier are aimed at improving the behaviour of students who are at risk of continuing challenging behaviour but do not require the Tier 3 high intensity interventions. Interventions include social skills learning groups, check in/check out mentoring programs, and behaviour education plans (OSEP Technical Assistance Center on Positive Behavioural Interventions and Supports, 2017). The level of effectiveness of these interventions can be used as part of the formal process to make decisions about increasing or decreasing the level of support provided to students. Tier 2 strategies should be effective for 15% of the students for whom Tier 1 interventions proved unsuccessful. A further 5% of students may require more intensive Tier 3 interventions (OSEP Technical Assistance Center on Positive Behavioural Interventions and Supports, 2017).

Tier 3

The third tier is known as the tertiary, or intensive tier. This tier is also concerned with reducing the prevalence of challenging behaviours that have not been successfully addressed by the efforts in the first two tiers. This tier encompasses individualised interventions such as functional behavioural assessment leading to the creation of an individualised behaviour support plan that includes: (a) prevention, (b) teaching, (c) positive reinforcement, (d) environmental manipulation to reduce natural rewards for problem behaviour, and (e) safety. Team-based or wraparound services, where a team of individual service providers collaborate to develop and implement a plan of support for the student, are implemented at this tier (OSEP Technical Assistance Center on Positive Behavioural Interventions and Supports, 2015). Formal data is collected on both the implementation of the behaviour support plan and the effect of the plan on student outcomes is collected and used to make decisions about intervention.

Implementation of PBIS is a process unto itself, and it can take years for full implementation to occur. According to the *PBIS Implementation Blueprint*, this is when the organisation has developed the "capacity to implement with greater internal (leadership team) levels of prompting, monitoring, and implementation feedback and less external TA" (OSEP Technical Assistance Center on Positive Behavioural Interventions and Supports, 2015, p. 25). Indicators of this include outcomes replicated across sites within the organisation, cost-effective resource management, fidelity of implementation, and all organisational structures in place and functioning effectively. Beyond full implementation, the organisation works to sustain, scale, and continuously improve their PBIS systems. There is a strong evidence base to support the use of PBIS system-wide to improve school climate, reduce problem behaviours, and combat bullying (Bradshaw, Koth, Thornton, & Leaf, 2009; Goldweber, Waasdorp, & Bradshaw, 2013; Horner et al., 2010).

Multi-tiered systems of support (MTSS)

Both RtI and PBIS have shared components. RtI is focused on supporting students in the area of academics, while Positive Behaviour Intervention and Support (PBIS) is used to support students in the area of behaviour and social-emotional needs. As both RtI and PBIS are tiered levels of services, the term multi-tiered systems of support (MTSS) has been used to present a framework which supports students in both academics and behaviour. MTSS has been described as a framework which uses instruction, assessment, intervention, and decision making in a tiered delivery system, as opposed to the focus of RtI, which some believe is for special education identification. For the purpose of this book, the authors will use McIntosh and Goodman's (2016) definition of MTSS:

> Integration of a number of multiple tiered systems into one coherent, strategically combined system meant to address multiple domains or content areas in education (e.g., literacy) and social-emotional competence.
>
> *(p. 13)*

A well formulated MTSS framework allows all students to be successful both academically and behaviourally. MTSS is the systematic implementation of interventions to meet the needs of students. It is not simply the application of RtI and PBIS but the synthesis of them.

Culturally responsive education

In order for MTSS systems to be responsive to the needs of all students, there needs to be an understanding of how culturally responsive education can be interwoven with the components of MTSS. Banks (2016) detailed how the culturally responsive education can be completed through five dimensions. The dimensions are (a) multicultural content integration, (b) knowledge construction, (c) prejudice reduction, (d) equity pedagogy, and (e) empowerment.

Multicultural content integration

Multicultural content integration targets what content is included in instruction, how the multicultural content should be integrated, and where in the curriculum the information will be added. Important aspects of content integration are the use of a variety of cultures and/or groups in the examples and data. The use of a wide range of groups to show and illustrate key points of instruction allows the educator to illuminate diversity in different ways. Teachers tend to use differences to highlight diversity. It is recognised that the type of systemic change envisioned by advocates of multicultural education may occur over time and with differing approaches to content and culture.

Beyond the dimensions of multicultural education, Banks (2016) delineated four approaches to providing multicultural education instruction. It should be noted that each of these approaches is valid and important in changing bias and underlying assumptions. The *contributions approach* is one used in many schools. Students are introduced to important people, holidays, and elements of different cultures. This is typically accomplished through celebrations, food, and other discrete methods. Cultural differences are experienced as an event, rather than an integral part of learning. The *additive approach* involves adding information about culture and cultural perspectives to the already existing and ongoing structure of a course. The fundamental objectives, purpose, and structure of the course remain unchanged in this approach. The *transformation approach* is a method for providing students with the opportunity to view concepts, issues, and events from the perspective of a diverse cultural and/or ethnic group. Methods in this approach require that the content and structure of the curriculum be changed to facilitate the deep learning of students. Finally, the *social action approach* involves what the name implies. Students learn to take action to solve issues and problems surrounding the discussion of cultural and racial differences.

Knowledge construction

Through appropriate knowledge construction, educators assist students with gaining a deeper understanding and investigate how implicit biases and assumptions exist. The knowledge construction process helps teachers to move to a different level. The teachers who utilise this process don't just provide students with the content they are teaching. They assist the students in working towards a greater depth of understanding related to that content. Specifically, the teachers help students learn, discover, and examine how cultural assumptions are applied in the content being taught. Additionally, students learn to look through the frames of reference and perspectives of the information that they are being given.

Understanding who is providing the information is an important piece of acquiring that information.

The knowledge construction process includes the instructional strategies (e.g., methods, activities, questioning approaches) that teacher uses to ensure students investigate the ways knowledge is constructed. Through this approach, students learn to understand how ethnicity, social class, ability, and gender influence what is being taught. Understanding how knowledge is constructed within all content areas and school expectations is important to help students develop their higher-order thinking skills, as well as empathy. Having students understand how knowledge is constructed is an important piece of their ability to construct their own knowledge. The result being students who are able to critically analyse information that they are given in the school and elsewhere in their lives.

Prejudice reduction

This dimension of multicultural education is focused on helping students learn democratic attitudes, values, and behaviours (Institute of Medicine and National Research Council, 2000; Oskamp, 2000; Van Ausdale & Feagin, 2001). Prejudice reduction involves educators strategically working with children to reduce the likelihood that the students will develop prejudicial beliefs. These strategies strive to characterise the students' racial attitudes and help them form demographic attitudes and values.

The goal of incorporating prejudice reduction strategies into the classroom is to develop positive, inclusive, and democratic attitudes towards other students and individuals of different races, ethnicities, genders, and ability. It is also meant to help students understand how ethnic, gender, or ability identity is influenced in by the attitudes and beliefs of the groups we encounter. Some characteristics of prejudice reduction that the students experience equal status in the school, students are cooperative rather than competitive, and these experiences are encouraged and directed by the adults (e.g., parents, educators, administrators).

Equity pedagogy

Equity pedagogy exists when teachers modify their teaching in order to increase the achievement of students from diverse racial, cultural, socioeconomic, and language groups. Ways that teachers achieve equity pedagogy include implementing a variety of teaching styles and approaches consistent with the range of learning styles within various cultural and ethnic groups. Equity pedagogy is achieved when teachers are able to modify their teaching practice to ensure that they are presenting content in a way that many students can achieve academically (Banks, 2015)

Empowering school culture

An empowering school culture involves restructuring the whole-school organisation and structure to ensure that all students experience equality (Banks, 2015).

This dimension of multicultural education requires that the school conduct an examination of the culture and organisation of the school system to identify the strengths and weaknesses of the system in relation to educational equity. The previous dimensions deal with different aspects of the culture and social system of the school.

When looking at developing a school that empowers students from all cultures and abilities, the entire system must be examined. This includes grouping practices, testing practices, labelling practices, sports participation, gaps in achievement, assessing for disabilities and giftedness, and seating patterns during lunch and recess breaks (Fuglei, 2014). Each of these practices have the potential to lend themselves to inequality in the system. Additionally, it is important that in addition to these practices, the behaviours and beliefs of educators, staff, and administration are also examined. This dimension centres around the school as a cultural and social system that serves students from diverse racial, ethnic, socioeconomic, language, and ability groups. This system examines the relationships that students develop with other students as well as with educators on the campus. These relationships must be based upon respect for cultural differences. These differences must be reflected in the school goals, norms, and practices. A school that empowers all of its students uses multicultural education and provides the teachers with the systems needed to make the empowerment possible.

MTSS and CRE integration

The combination of RtI and PBIS into one systematic framework results in a MTSS (Office of Learning Supports at Colorado Department of Education, 2015). While this is a step in the right direction, there is still a glaring omission, in that the current status of these models may not take into account needs of all students; neither the separate frameworks nor the combined contain direction on how to implement their evidence-based strategies in a culturally responsive manner. We suggest a model that combines the multi-tiered systems of support (namely PBIS and RtI) in a culturally responsive manner. The multi-tiered culturally responsive system of support (MTCRSS) is a strengths-based model that values student differences rather than viewing them as deficits. The model is grounded in the theoretical frameworks that underpin PBIS, RtI, and CRE, which are discussed in detail in Chapter 2. Therefore, a detailed description of MTCRSS and its grounding can be found there.

The authors of this volume seek to provide readers with the means to implement the strategies within the combined multi-tiered system of support through the use of culturally responsive pedagogy. This chapter has provided an overview of RtI and PBIS models as part of MTSS and an overview of culturally responsive pedagogy. Chapter 2 aims to build upon this by exploring the theoretical frameworks of each and present a combined RtI and PBIS multi-tiered system of support that is culturally responsive and inclusive of at-risk students with specific needs. The remaining chapters will describe a variety of diverse populations and their specific support needs, provide strategies for working with students in these populations, and suggest ways that schools can build an inclusive culture that is culturally competent and student- and family-focused by incorporating the MTCRSS model.

References

Banks, J. A. (2016). *Cultural diversity and education* (6th ed.). New York, NY: Routledge.

Bradshaw, C. P., Koth, C. W., Thornton, L. A., & Leaf, P. J. (2009). Altering school climate through school-wide positive behavioural interventions and supports: Findings from a group-randomized effectiveness trial. *Prevention Science, 10*(2), 100–115.

Fuchs, D., & Deshler, D. D. (2007). What we need to know about responsiveness to intervention (and shouldn't be afraid to ask). *Learning Disabilities Research & Practice, 22*(2), 129–136.

Fuglei, M. (2014, June 11). *Culturally responsive teaching: Empowering students through respect.* Retrieved from http://education.cu-portland.edu/blog/news/culturally-responsive-teachingempowering-students-through-respect/

Gay and Lesbian Equality Network (GLEN). (2016). *'Being LGBT in school' A resource for post-primary schools to prevent homophobic and transphobic bullying and support LGBT students.* Retrieved from www.education.ie/en/Publications/Education-Reports/Being-LGBT-in-School.pdf

Gagnon, J. C., & Richards, C. (2008). *Making the right turn: A guide about improving transition outcomes of youth involved in the juvenile corrections system.* Washington, DC: National Collaborative on Workforce and Disability for Youth, Institute for Educational Leadership.

Goldweber, A., Waasdorp, T. E., & Bradshaw, C. P. (2013). Examining the link between forms of bullying behaviours and perceptions of safety and belonging among secondary school students. *Journal of School Psychology, 51*(4), 469–485. doi:10.1016/j.jsp.2013.04.004

Gunn, B., Biglan, A., Smolkowski, K., & Ary, D. (2000). The efficacy of supplemental instruction in decoding skills for Hispanic and non-Hispanic students in early elementary school. *Journal of Special Education, 34*(2), 90–103.

Haager, D., Klinger, J., & Vaughn, S. (2007). *Evidence-based reading practices for response to intervention.* Baltimore, MD: Brookes.

Harn, B. A., Kame'enui, E. J., & Simmons, D. C. (2007). Essential features of interventions for kindergarten students most in need of accelerated learning: The nature and role of the third tier in a prevention model for kindergarten students. In D. Haager, J. Klinger, & S. Vaughn (Eds.), *Evidence-based reading practices for response to intervention* (pp. 161–184). Baltimore, MD: Brookes.

Horner, R. H., Sugai, G., & Anderson, C. M. (2010). Examining the evidence base for school-wide positive behaviour support. *Focus on Exceptionality, 42*(8), 1–14.

Institute of Medicine and National Research Council. (2000). *Improving intergroup relations among youth: Summary of a research workshop.* Washington, DC: The National Academies Press. https://doi.org/10.17226/9754.

Leone, P. E., & Mayer, M. J. (2004). Safety, diversity, and disability: "Goodness of fit" and the complexities of the school environment. In M. J. Furlong, M. P. Bates, & P. Kingery (Eds.), *Bet practices in school-based threat assessment.* Hauppauge, NY: Nova Science.

McIntosh, K., & Goodman, S. (2016). *Integrated multi-tiered systems of support: Blending RTI and PBIS.* New York: Guilford Press.

National Research Center on Learning Disabilities (NRCLD). (2004). *Understanding response to intervention in learning disabilities determination.* Retrieved from http://www.nrcld.org

O'Connor, R. E., & Sanchez, V. (2011). Responsiveness to intervention models for reducing reading difficulties and identifying learning disability. In J. M. Kauffman & D. P. Hallahan (Eds.), *Handbook of special education* (pp. 703–715). New York, NY: Routledge.

Office of Learning Supports at Colorado Department of Education. (2015). *What is MTSS?* Retrieved from https://www.cde.state.co.us/mtss/whatismtss

OSEP Technical Assistance Center on Positive Behavioural Interventions and Supports. (2015, October). *Positive Behavioural Interventions and Supports (PBIS) implementation blueprint: Part 1 – foundations and supporting information.* Eugene, OR: University of Oregon. Retrieved from www.pbis.org

OSEP Technical Assistance Center on Positive Behavioural Interventions and Supports. (2017). *Positive behavioural interventions & supports* [Website]. Retrieved from www.pbis.org

Oskamp, S. (Ed.). (2000). *Reducing prejudice and discrimination* (The Claremont Symposium on Applied Social Psychology). Mahwah, NJ: Lawrence Erlbaum Associates Publishers.

Quinn, M. M., Rutherford, R. B., Leone, P. E., Osher, D, M., & Poirer, J. M. (2005). Youth with disabilities in juvenile corrections: A national survey. *Exceptional Children, 71,* 339–345.

Shaywitz, B. A., Shaywitz, S. E., Blachman, B. A., Pugh, K. R., Fulbright, R. K., Skudlarski, P., . . . Gore, J. C. (2004). Developmental of left occipito-temporal systems for skilled reading in children after a phonologically-based intervention. *Biological Psychiatry, 55,* 926–933.

Simmons, D. C., Kame'enui, E. J., Coyne, M. D., & Chard, D. (2002). Effective strategies for teaching beginning reading. In E. J. Kame'enui, D. W. Carnine, R. C. Dixon, D. C. Simmons, & M. D. Coyne (Eds.), *Effective teaching strategies that accommodate diverse learners* (2nd ed., pp. 53–92). Columbus, OH: Merrill.

Sugai, G., & Simonsen, B. (2012). *Positive behavioral interventions and supports: History, defining features, and misconceptions.* Center for PBIS & Center for Positive Behavioral Interventions and Supports, University of Connecticut. Retrieved January 14, 2014 from www.pbis.org/common/pbisresources/publications/PBIS_revisited_June19r_2012.pdf

Van Ausdale, D., & Feagin, J. R. (2001). *The first R: How children learn race and racism.* Guilford, CT: Rowman & Littlefield.

VanDerHeyden, A., Witt, J., & Gilbertson, D. (2007). A multi-year evaluation of the effects of a Response to Intervention (RtI) model on identification of children for special education. *Journal of School Psychology, 45,* 225–256.

Vaughn, S., Linan-Thompson, S., & Hickman, P. (2003). Response to instruction as a means of identifying students with reading/learning disabilities. *Exceptional Children, 69,* 391–409.

Vellutino, F., Scanlon, D., Sipay, E., Small, S., Pratt, A., Chen, R., & Denckla, M. B. (1996). Cognitive profiles of difficult-to-remediate and readily remediated poor readers: Early intervention as a vehicle for distinguishing between cognitive and experiential deficits as basic causes of specific reading disability. *Journal of Educational Psychology, 88,* 601–638.

Wanzek, J., & Vaughn, S. (2007). Research-based implications from extensive early reading interventions. *School Psychology Review, 36,* 541–561.

2

RESEARCH AND THEORY FRAMING THE MULTI-TIERED CULTURALLY RESPONSIVE SYSTEM OF SUPPORT MODEL

Introduction

Just as a house needs a solid frame, models of educational practice benefit from having a solid grounding in theory and science. A theoretical framework provides a rationale for the relationships among the components of the model, and science provides evidence that the components of the model will be effective (Breakwell, Hammon, Fife-Schaw, & Smith, 2007). Theory supports research by allowing for the examination of a problem and developing hypotheses and/or solutions. Thus, a solid theoretical framework gives a frame of reference for the design of a research study and any resulting models (Creswell, 2009). Overall, the theoretical framework serves as a guide to systematically identify logical, precisely defined relationships among variables. A sound theoretical framework that is substantiated by research can be used to support the use of the model it grounds (Breakwell et al., 2007).

The multi-tiered culturally responsive system of support (MTCRSS) (see Figure 2.1) is a combination of existing models and theories, so the theory and science underpinning each must first be looked at in isolation. Positive Behaviour Interventions and Supports (PBIS) has its roots in behavioural theory and the science of applied behaviour analysis (ABA). Response to Intervention (RtI) is grounded in constructivist learning theory and the science of data-based decision making and the implementation of evidence-based practices. These models have been combined into a multi-tiered system of support (MTSS), which is often informed by theory of action and theory of change, along with implementation science. There is a dearth of scientific evidence supporting the use of culturally responsive practices, but cultural responsiveness is strongly supported by constructionist learning and universal design for learning theories. These theoretical frameworks are explored, and the resulting model is described.

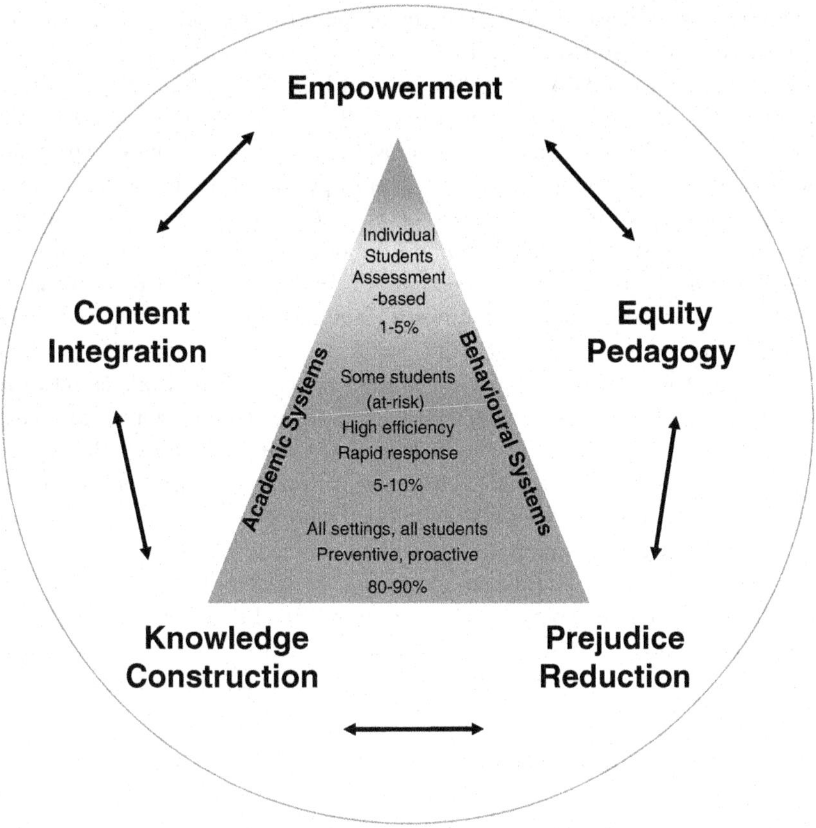

FIGURE 2.1 Multi-tiered culturally responsive system of support (MTCRSS)

Theories underpinning PBIS

The system of Positive Behavioural Interventions and Supports (PBIS) is solidly framed by applied behaviour analysis (ABA). Applied behaviour analysis takes a behavioural perspective that focuses on what is observable and measurable. The underlying assumption is that behaviour is influenced by the environment; therefore, to change behaviour, one must first assess the functional relationship between a targeted behaviour and the environment (Cooper, Heron, & Heward, 2013). Replacement behaviours that serve the same function as the misbehaviour are then developed, along with an intervention and support plan.

ABA is based on the work of B. F. Skinner, the founding father of behaviourism, which is an authoritarian approach to behaviour change. Behaviours are seen as observable, functional, purposeful, and measurable. Environments, such as the classroom, should be changed to support students in improving their behaviour. ABA is founded upon five basic principles: (a) antecedent control, (b) positive reinforcement, (c) negative reinforcement, (d) punishment, and (e) extinction (De Nobile, Lyons, & Arthur-Kelly, 2017).

PBIS goes beyond ABA to include tenets of Brofenbrenner's ecological theory of human development (Bronfenbrenner, 1989), in that it goes beyond the individual child to address factors in the microsystem and mesosystem to explain and intervene with inappropriate behaviours. Simply put, a child's microsystem includes family, close friends, religion, teachers, peers, school courses, workplace, employers, and co-workers. The mesosystem, on the other hand, consists of the interactions between the microsystems. Examples of this in relation to PBIS would be home-school communication, educational planning, support planning and transition planning.

PBIS emphasises, within a multi-tiered support system framework: (a) measurable outcomes, (b) evidence-based practices, (c) implementation systems, and (d) data for decision making (OSEP Technical Assistance Center on Positive Behavioural Interventions and Supports, 2015). These foundations blend together to form the PBIS pyramid that many are familiar with (see Figure 1.1). The pyramid represents a three-tiered system of support that is based on the use of practical, evidence-based interventions that are committed to improving the lifestyle outcomes of students. See Chapter 1 for a more detailed explanation of PBIS. PBIS is often implemented in conjunction with RtI and combined into one framework to more seamlessly meet the needs of a diverse population of students (Fuchs & Deshler, 2007).

Theories underpinning RtI

RtI is a tiered system of evidence-based practices and interventions to support instruction in a comprehensive integrated manner (Ridgeway, Price, Simpson, & Rose, 2011). Data-based decision making is used to guide interventions, which are based on students' responses to instruction in the general education classroom. Like PBIS, RtI is theoretically grounded in research-based practices, but also akin to PBIS, RtI can be viewed through a sociocultural lens (Drame & Xu, 2008). Drame and Xu's sociocultural view also aligns well with the ecological theory of human development (Bronfenbrenner, 1989) in that they believe that factors such as community, school, classroom, and teachers impact all tiers of the RtI model and student achievement. They posit that it is important to examine the cultural and environmental conditions of the context where the risk factors occur. Family and community contexts are interwoven throughout all of the tiers of RTI, as are group contexts. Families should be included as partners in the RTI process, particularly when it comes to finding solutions to their children's difficulties. This links well to the micro- and mesosystems in Bronfenbrenner's ecological theory.

From a sociocultural perspective, it is important to assess the social, cultural, and community context, in light of daily interactions. These interactions affect students' interactions in school and influence school attitudes, policies, and practices. Differences in the district and school context such as school socioeconomic status, special education referral practices, teacher quality, and financial resources can advantage or disadvantage child development (Klinger & Edwards, 2006). Classroom and teacher contexts must also be considered, as they influence the student's behaviour as part of the class and with his or her interactions with other students (Drame & Xu, 2008).

RtI is also grounded in constructivist learning theory, which addresses how learning occurs through accommodation and assimilation. Accommodation is reframing new experiences into what is already known, particularly when these experiences do not operate within the familiar context. Assimilation, on the other hand, is when the individual incorporates new experiences into the old. The role of the teacher in this theory is that of a facilitator, to assist students in becoming critical thinkers who come to their own conclusions (John-Steiner & Mahn, 1996). The teacher must create a learning experience that is tailored to the needs of students; this is well aligned with the tiered system of intervention in RtI.

RtI implementation has merged with PBIS and school improvement or reform efforts and into multi-tiered systems of support (MTSS) (Jimerson, Burns, & VanDerHeyden, 2016). It must be noted however, that MTSS is not just the joining of the two systems; it involves the application of implementation science and the integration of student support frameworks into one coherent system.

Theories underpinning MTSS

A MTSS is a "whole-school, data-driven, prevention-based framework for improving learning outcomes for every student through a layered continuum of evidence-based practices and systems" (Office of Learning Supports at Colorado Department of Education, 2015, p. 1). The integration of RtI and PBIS into one systematic framework results in a MTSS. MTSS has six essential components: (a) shared leadership, (b) data-based decision making, (c) a layered continuum of supports, (d) an evidence-based approach to instruction, intervention, and assessment, (e) universal screening and progress monitoring, and (f) partnerships among the school, families, and the community (Office of Learning Supports at Colorado Department of Education, 2015). The formation of leadership teams at each level of the system (school and district, for example) is crucial to the success of implementation across all levels of the framework. The function of these teams is to create a common vision and use common language to define desired outcomes, use data-based problem solving and decision making, and conduct an ongoing evaluation of progress. These activities are well aligned with the tenets of implementation science and theories of action and change.

Implementation science

According to the Fogarty International Center (2017), implementation science is the study of the adoption and integration of evidence-based practices, interventions, and policies into everyday practice. This science originated in the field of health care but has direct application to educational MTSS. According to implementation science, the planned outcomes of evidence-based practice are significantly affected by the fidelity and fluency with which they are implemented (Blase & Fixsen, 2013). This highlights the importance of teacher professional development and support and the evaluation of implementation practices and systems.

Barrett, Eber, and Weist (2013) point out that there are a variety of factors linked to problematic or failed implementation, including lack of funding, poorly trained implementers, failure of data-based decision-making systems, and a lack of alignment between intended and actual outcomes. In education, this may result in an increase in reactive and exclusionary discipline, inequity for culturally and linguistically diverse (CALD) students, poor classroom and school climate, and student dissatisfaction (Dix, Slee, Lawson, & Keeves, 2012). Implementation science can assist schools in operationalising and implementing an MTSS. Implementation science uses a series of questions to guide these activities: (a) What are the needs and intended outcomes? (b) Have the most appropriate evidence-based practices been chosen? (c) Are the practices contextualised to the setting and culture? (d) Has support for implementation been developed? and (e) Is continuous monitoring and planning in place? (Barrett et al., 2013). These questions can be used as guiding principles and for self-assessment for action planning, which can be grounded in theory of change and theory of action.

Theory of change

Theory of change has its beginnings in community-based change initiatives but is applicable to educational change through MTSS implementation (Anderson, 2004; Organizational Research Services, 2004). Theory of change is basically an understanding of how a social, political, economic, and/or cultural change happens. Talpin and Clark (2012, p. 1) describe theory of change as:

> A rigorous yet participatory process whereby groups and stakeholders in a planning process articulate their long-term goals and identify the conditions they believe have to unfold for those goals to be met. These conditions are modelled as desired outcomes and arranged graphically in a causal framework.

Theory of change is especially applicable to MTSS, as it describes the interventions, program, or framework that are used to deliver the desired outcomes. Each intervention is mapped to an outcome to ensure that it is appropriate and will work to test hypotheses about which actions will produce the best outcomes (Talpin & Clark, 2012).

The first step in theory of change is to identify the organisation's long-term goals, then backwards map from the goals by determining what is necessary to achieve that goal and why. Organizational Research Services (2004) posits that impact, influence, and leverage outcomes can be achieved if the core capacities that are necessary to achieve the outcomes are functioning well. The interventions are then strategically chosen based on the desired change. Indicators should be developed to measure progress on the desired outcomes and evaluate how the system is working overall (Anderson, 2004). One of the benefits of using change theory to frame MTSS is that it can be used for both planning and evaluation.

Theory of action

A theory of action explains how a particular program or initiative contributes to the change process and is informed by the broader theory of change. Sugai (2017) suggests that theory of action can act as a guide to illustrate the connection between strategies needed to answer specific questions and to achieve desired outcomes. In other words, to achieve a particular outcome, a particular action is necessary. Theory of action is based on a set of underlying and supporting testable hypotheses or a logic model and stresses the importance of the ability to justify the hypothesis, outcome interpretations, practice, and systems decisions. When applied to organisations, a theory of action is a set of assumptions about how the organisation can be moved from its current state to a desired future state.

When applied to MTSS, theory of action can guide educational leaders to improve teaching, learning, and leadership practice. The University of Washington Center for Educational Leadership (2015) has created a tool to help educators design a theory of action that explains the changes and interventions they will implement to improve teaching and learning. The authors of the tool suggest that it is crucial to have a clear picture of what is working and what is not working for students and that problems of student learning and problems in teaching and educational leadership must be identified. This analysis is then used to generate a theory of action. MTSS combines the components of implementation science, theory of change, and theory of action to positively impact a school's environment, climate, learning, teaching, and leadership practices.

Culturally responsive education

Scholars believe that in order for there to be changes to education, practice must acknowledge that students come to school with different backgrounds and needs. Therefore, the proposed framework infuses the tenets of MTSS with culturally responsive education practice. Given the trends in population growth, and the increase of diverse groups of learners in public schools, researchers have been interested in culturally responsive pedagogy (CRP) and its impact on school-wide practices (Gay, 2013).

CRP is the acknowledgement that the culture of students of colour has long been unrepresented and unconsidered in instructional planning and educational research. CRP strives to infuse the cultures of these students into the academic and social aspects of school in order to empower students by making meaningful cultural connections (Vavrus, 2008). Advocates of CRP come from differing disciplines and backgrounds, but there are specific points of agreement. There is agreement that CRP is a mechanism for reforming education and instruction so that cultural pluralism can be fostered and realised as a means of acknowledging the unique ethnic identities of the larger population (Gay, 2013).

CRP can and should be infused in all content areas of instruction in public schools. In order to achieve this, school programs, policies, and practices will need to be changed. Diversity is valued, including the recognition that content, structures, and practices will potentially be different in each setting. Decision making is configured differently so that all stakeholders are involved and decisions are less hierarchical and more democratic. Ultimately, incorporating CRP requires changes on all levels, (i.e., community, administrative, school) (Gay, 2013). Similar to RtI, CRP has its foundations in offshoots of constructivist theory, in the forms of constructionism learning theory and theory of multidimensional multicultural education.

Constructionism learning theory

Constructionism builds upon the tenets of constructivist theory to view earning as a reconstruction rather than as a transmission of knowledge (Sabelli, 2008). Constructionism also assumes that learning is most effective when it takes place through an activity that results in a meaningful product (Papert & Harel, 1991). This assumption is closely linked with CRP, as an individual's perception of what is meaningful is inextricably tied to his or her culture.

Constructionism supports student-centred discovery learning, such as that which is found in project-based learning. This pedagogy supports students' learning about a topic by suggesting several problems and encouraging them to construct knowledge via solving them. This problem-solving approach should be delivered via an authentic task matched to students' cognitive abilities and the problem (Hmelo-Silver & Barrows, 2006). The teacher's role is that of a facilitator rather than an instructor, assisting students in reaching an understanding through the creation of hands-on activities. This theory supports the five interactive dimensions of multicultural education posited by Banks (2016).

Theory of multidimensional multicultural education

Banks (2015) describes five interactive dimensions of multicultural education. These are important starting points for CRP. First, there must be an empowering school culture and social structure. All aspects of the school, (i.e., instruction, content, extracurricular activities, grouping, labelling, achievement gaps, and interactions of staff and students), must be examined and analysed to assure that ALL students are empowered. Second, teachers must use an equity pedagogy, modifying planning, delivery, and evaluation to include all of the students in their class. Third, teachers integrate the content. Teachers use examples that represent a variety of cultures to illustrate key concepts, principles, and theories in teaching instructional content. Fourth, teachers employ effective methods to facilitate the knowledge construction process for students. Students are provided with opportunities to understand, investigate, and determine ways that commonly accepted cultural biases effect and permeate all aspects of society. Teachers and students examine and analyse the construction of knowledge within a content area. Finally, the culmination of the previous four dimensions is the reduction of prejudice. The hope is that through integrally and authentically examining cultural and racial bias that permeates the school culture and content, students, teachers, and other school personnels' racial attitudes may be modified. It is recognised the type of systemic change envisioned by advocates of CRP may occur over time and with differing approaches to content and culture.

Universal design for learning theory

It would be remiss to not include an operational theory. The foundational purpose of universal design for learning (UDL) theory is to achieve equity pedagogy. UDL is an educational framework based on research in the learning sciences that guides the development of flexible learning environments (CAST, 2011a). It defined as:

> a set of principles for curriculum development that give all individuals equal opportunities to learn. UDL provides a blueprint for creating instructional goals, methods, materials, and assessments that work for everyone – not a single, one-size-fits-all solution but rather flexible approaches that can be customized and adjusted for individual needs.

CAST (2011b) details the three principles that guide UDL: (a) provide multiple means of representation; (b) provide multiple means of action and expression; and (c) provide multiple means of engagement. These three principles and the UDL model are now widely accepted and recommended as part of different teaching models, including the popular differentiated instruction model (Tomlinson, 2008). The principles fit very well in the equity pedagogy and content integration dimensions, as they can be used to guide teachers in designing instruction that meets the academic, behavioural, social, and cultural needs of all of the students in their classes.

Universal design for learning has received attention because designing instruction in this manner benefits all students. UDL involves planning environments and teaching materials in such a way that they are accessible to all individuals. Using the UDL framework and including experiences from diverse populations underpins CRP, while the basic tenets of UDL align well with the primary universal tiers of both PBIS and RtI. We propose that the systems of student support described earlier can be combined into a single system that incorporates the philosophies of all three to provide teachers with a single system that can guide them in providing culturally responsive instructional and behavioural support for all of their students.

The multi-tiered culturally responsive system of support

Scholars and practitioners alike have begun combining the multi-tiered systems of support found in RtI and PBIS into a single system. While this makes sense, Sugai and Horner (2009) caution that the two systems cannot simply be combined. A school-wide assessment should be conducted to determine: (a) what the strengths are, (b) what programs or practices should be eliminated because data shows they are ineffective, (c) what programs and practices should be modified because they are not culturally or contextually appropriate, and (d) what programs or practices can be downsized because they have already produced the desired results or combined with another initiative with a similar outcome goal. The focus on contextual and cultural appropriateness highlights the need for an MTSS that not only combines academic and behavioural systems of support but also does this in a culturally responsive manner. The multi-tiered culturally responsive system of support (MTCRSS) is a model that infuses cultural responsiveness into MTSS.

The idea of MTSS being culturally responsive has been explored briefly by Sugai and Horner (2009), and Bianco and Harris (2016) discussed the need for a culturally responsive strengths-based RtI model, but in relation to identifying the gifted potential of students who were English language learners. They encouraged practitioners to value the cultural beliefs and practices of these students, rather than viewing them as deficits. They further suggested that the success of a culturally responsive strengths-based RtI model is dependent on teachers' knowledge, skills, and dispositions; they must change their deficit thinking to dynamic thinking.

The MTCRSS infuses Banks' (2015) five interactive dimensions of multicultural education across all three tiers of academic and behavioural interventions and supports (see Figure 2.1). This results in a model that can guide educators in providing a continuum of culturally responsive academic and behavioural interventions and supports to diverse populations of students. A description of the model and its three tiers of support follow.

Overview of MTCRSS

There are ten basic operating principles to guide implementation of the system:

1 Use data-based problem solving and decision making.
2 Data is used to identify culturally relevant and realistically achievable goals, expectations, outcomes.
3 Key concepts, competencies, and student outcomes for academic and behavioural development are culturally responsive, targeted, and modelled across all three tiers.
4 The adoption of culturally responsive evidence-based practices and interventions to support the achievement of academic and behavioural goals, objectives, and outcomes.
5 Resources are organised to support accurate, fluent, and sustained implementation through opportunity, capacity, and resources.
6 There are clear expectations for performance, balanced with the use of student choice to maximise student engagement and motivation.
7 The use of culturally responsive pedagogy that promotes active engagement and opportunities to respond.
8 Logical progression of instruction from easier to more complex concepts.

9 Teachers provide students with opportunities to practice new skills, both academic and behavioural, with varied degrees of teacher support and learning contexts.
10 Mastery of academic and behavioural outcomes is monitored so that instructional adaptations, modelling, and corrective feedback occur when necessary.

At least 80% of staff must buy into implementation for two years in order for it to be effective (Stoiber & Gettinger, 2015). Part of this buy-in involves the mentality that "all students in the school are everyone's responsibility". This includes students with special needs as well as English language learners. Professional development is essential and must be ongoing rather than one-off sessions. This includes ongoing support, which is continuous and embedded in the school routines. It must be focused on building fluency and implementation fidelity rather than just disseminating information. Professional development should also be adapted to the culture and characteristics of the local context and be structured in a way that provides continuous organisational support for onsite coaching, monitoring, and reinforcement.

Similar to RtI and PBIS, MTCRSS is organised into three tiers. Tier 1 is primary prevention and should successfully support 85% of students in meeting their academic and behavioural outcomes. Tier 2 is secondary prevention that supplements Tier 1 to enhance student behaviour and learning. Practices at this tier are effective in supporting a further 10% of the student population. Tier 3 contains tertiary supports and interventions and uses more intensive interventions to reach the final 5% of struggling students. Movement between the tiers is fluid, for example, students may be in Tier 2 for behaviour but remain in Tier 1 academically. Support is downgraded in intensity when students meet outcomes and extra support is no longer necessary.

Primary prevention (Tier 1)

Tier 1 is meant to support the cultural, academic, and behavioural needs of all students at the school. Simply stated, it is culturally responsive and systematic evidence-based instruction and classroom management for all students delivered in general education settings by general education teachers. Ecological adjustments are made school- and classroom-wide to support positive behaviour (Stoiber & Gettinger, 2015). The dimensions of culturally responsive education (Banks, 2015) come into play across all of the tiers, but it is important to form a solid basis in Tier 1.

The stakeholders of the school, which include school leaders, teachers, other staff, students, parents, and the community, must form a team to make important decisions about the goals, expectations, and outcomes in regard to the model (Sugai & Horner, 2009). A good place to begin is with a comprehensive assessment of all areas of the school – ecological, academic, behavioural, and social – to collect data that can be used to identify *empowering* school culture and social structure. As stated earlier, this equates to examining content, pedagogy, extracurricular activities, and interactions of staff and students. It is also crucial to look at the school's procedures for grouping and labelling students and how achievement gaps and referrals for special education services are conducted. Universal screenings of student progress academically and behaviourally are conducted three times a year to identify students who need additional support (NASP, 2009). These screenings ensure that all students have access to the general education curriculum regardless of educational and behavioural needs, race, culture, or socioeconomic status. The assessments should include culturally responsive behavioural checklists and curriculum-based measurements.

It is important that a validated curriculum is chosen and used in each content area. These curricula must have evidence that academic performance will improve when they are implemented with fidelity (Lane, Menzies, Ennis, & Bezdek, 2013). The teacher's role here is to do this, while at the same time employing *equity pedagogy* and *content integration* to differentiate their instruction to meet the academic, behavioural, and cultural needs of a diverse student population. This is done through the provision of multiple means of representation, action and expression, and engagement. These means should always include examples that represent a variety of cultures, so that all students feel included. *Knowledge construction* is an important part of culturally responsive curriculum implementation. Students learn how content area subject matter is constructed from diverse racial and social class perspectives rather than solely from the dominant Euro-American models.

Tier 1 may include social supports such as evidence-based character development programs to teach social skills or prevent violence. These should fit the particular needs of the school such as decreasing bullying or increasing social skills (Lane et al., 2013). Although the *reduction of prejudice* should be a result of cultural responsiveness being infused into the Tier 1 screening and implementation activities, character development programs can also be used to give students a voice in the discussion and examination of cultural and racial bias.

Behaviourally, Tier 1 of the MTCRSS is strongly aligned with the PBIS framework and includes the provision of three to five universal expectations for student conduct. These are determined by collecting data from all building staff about what behaviours they think students need to have to be successful in all parts of the school. The expectations are explicitly taught, incorporating opportunities for students to practice and receive coaching and reinforcement through behaviour-specific praise. Depending on the needs of the students, this may include a school-wide or classroom token economy where a token is given with the praise (Lane et al., 2013). Teachers proactively teach and encourage students to meet the behavioural expectations. Although it may sound as if this would take time from academic instruction, it will, in reality, decrease the amount of instructional time teachers lose while attending to problem behaviours.

Secondary prevention for some (Tier 2)

Tier 2 is implemented in the general education classroom and designed via collaboration with various stakeholders, including the student and family. Tier 2 supports typically take the form of small group interventions. These interventions include native language support as well as valuing language and culture (Bianco & Harris, 2016). The school MTCRSS team identifies what resources are already available at the school that can be used for Tier 2 supports and then adds more if necessary. Examples of Tier 2 academic interventions include repeated readings to improve oral fluency, increased practice opportunities in literacy and numeracy, targeted instruction with explicit instruction and modelling, increased teaching for generalisation, guided instruction, more daily review activities, and study skills groups. Social interventions include social skills groups and conflict resolution groups. Behavioural supports are more individually focused and include contracts, self-monitoring, and check in/check out systems, modelling, guided practice, coaching, corrective feedback, peer-mediation, and self-monitoring (Lane et al., 2013). Overall, the supports in this tier include more exposure, more time, and more opportunities to learn.

Tier 2 is not meant to replace the evidence-based core curricula delivered in Tier 1; rather, it should supplement and enhance student learning. Team members consider students' language, experiences, preferred ways of interacting, and home practices and integrate these factors into intervention development and both formative and summative progress monitoring. Tier 2 intervention is of particular importance in kindergarten and may prevent the need for more intensive intervention in the future. In secondary school, Tier 2 intervention is focused on remediation and content-specific recovery.

The short-term goal of Tier 2 supports is for students to pass their courses, while graduation is the long-term goal. Teachers provide students with more frequent reinforcement for meeting expectations and instruction in and opportunities to practice academic, behavioural, or social skills. This tier typically includes 6–20 weeks of intervention. At the end of the predetermined intervention period, students can receive more Tier 2 intervention, discontinue Tier 2 intervention, or move to more intensive intervention at Tier 3 (Stoiber & Gettinger, 2015). Movement between the tiers is determined through data-based decision making. When conducting student assessments, it is of great importance to take into account students' level of acculturation and recognise that cultural differences may impact student achievement and behaviour.

Tier 3: tertiary prevention for a few

Tier 3 interventions are customised for individual students with multiple risk factors who are struggling in multiple areas and are still not meeting outcomes despite receiving Tier 1 and Tier 2 supports. Tier 3 requires more time and resources because these interventions are implemented by an expert, such as a reading specialist or special education teacher. Progress monitoring is also more frequent to enable better response to student needs. Due to their high academic, social, and/or behavioural support needs, students that need the intensive support of this tier will probably require multiple years of this level of support (Stoiber & Gettinger, 2015).

Tier 3 contains the most intensive interventions; most are individual strategies. Behavioural interventions at this level are typically based on functional behaviour assessment. The data from the assessment is used to design a multicomponent support plan targeting several variables. Evidence-based interventions are matched to functions and include token economies, positive and negative consequences, and the extinction of inappropriate behaviours. Academic interventions include special education services, evidence-based interventions. Intervention effectiveness should be monitored closely.

Cultural responsiveness at this tier involves consideration of not only what supports students receive but who provides them and where they are provided (Klinger & Edwards, 2006). In the best-case scenario, this may mean that supports such as scaffolded instruction are provided in the general education classroom, by special and general educators, as well as specialists in English language acquisition.

Implications for practice

Role of the team

The importance of strong teams that will implement MTCRSS cannot be understated (Morales-James, Lopez, Wilkins, & Fergus, n.d.). All school staff, but particularly educators, must examine the cultural lens from which they practice and make decisions to strengthen cultural responsiveness and decrease the vulnerability of culturally and linguistically diverse students. Areas to be examined and improved include tracking, exclusionary discipline practices, the curriculum, and quality of instructional supports of both teachers and students. Morales-James et al. (n.d.) presented the following suggestions as helpful in developing and implementing a culturally responsive system:

1. Define the purpose of the team and make its focus on developing teachers rather than changing students. This includes using equitable language and analysing trends that identify students that are struggling academically or behaviourally and investigating how this may be caused by misinterpretation based on their at-risk status.
2. Use "master teachers" as coaches to improve teaching and management practices. These coaches can model best practices, observe teachers, and give feedback.
3. School leaders attend instructional planning meetings to ensure that plans promote a culturally responsive culture across all tiers.
4. Implement a culturally responsive problem-solving model to determine whether cultural conflict and/or a deficit model is at the root of poor student outcomes.
5. Cultural considerations must be written into problem-solving models.
6. Staff must acknowledge students' prior knowledge and lived experiences, recognise their strengths, and value student and family cultural norms.

7 Parents and students should have a voice in decision-making processes.
8 Recognise that the rate of student progress varies, and culture is one factor that impacts this. Culturally responsive practice acknowledges that difference does not necessarily equate with disability.

Role of the teacher

Student data are used to evaluate the effectiveness of interventions and supports used across the three tiers, so teachers need to develop an increased understanding of what data to collect and how to collect it, as well as how to use it to guide decision making. This includes movement between tiers (Stoiber & Gettinger, 2015). Students accessing and exiting Tier 2 and 3 supports are examined periodically in terms of student group representation for patterns of disproportionality. Consistent overrepresentation of any specific student group requiring Tier 2 and/or Tier 3 supports is addressed by strengthening the responsiveness of Tier 1 or Tier 2 instruction

Fidelity of the model is dependent upon treatment integrity, accurate identification of student eligibility for each level, and fidelity of implementation of data systems, treatments, and structures. This requires that schools provide shared planning time for collaborative teacher teams, scheduling of time blocks where special educators and other specialists are able to co-teach in general education classrooms with appropriate frequency in order to fully support students who require tertiary intervention, and that ongoing professional learning addresses the needs for educators to build their collaborative and culturally responsive teaching practices (Klinger & Edwards, 2006). Lane et al. (2013) recommends practice-based professional development, which includes opportunities to engage in active learning and to practice the skills being taught. This is most effective when teachers from the same school with the same learning goals learn together and are given feedback.

Research-based strategies

Basic behaviour strategies and instructional pedagogy should be looked at first before considering Tier 2 or 3 support. Instructional organisation is a major factor in student behaviour and achievement. Differentiation, UDL, and student choice are all evidence-based practices that are culturally responsive and maximise engagement while minimising inappropriate behaviour (Lane et al., 2013). Class-wide behavioural practices include active supervision, teacher proximity, behaviour-specific praise, and increased opportunities to respond. Teachers can implement antecedent-based strategies, which involve changing the environment to meet the needs of students. Pre-correction involves the identification of problem areas, activities, and times when misbehaviour is likely to occur and then modifying the environment to promote success. This includes providing prompts and opportunities for behavioural rehearsal. Individual strategies are often based on a functional behavioural assessment and its resulting behaviour intervention plan. These involve choosing a replacement behaviour and withholding reinforcement for inappropriate behaviour while reinforcing the presence of the replacement behaviour.

Teachers should screen their students for academic proficiency levels, behavioural performance, and work completion. These data can then be aggregated to determine the risk levels of the students. If most of the students are at moderate and high risk, the teacher should then look at what changes can be made in pedagogy and behaviour management before considering Tier 2 and 3 supports. For some teachers, this identification will be enough, while others may need professional development with onsite coaching and performance feedback to strengthen their skills.

Conclusion

The MTCRSS model is a system that espouses data-based problem solving and decision making to identify culturally relevant and realistically achievable goals, expectations, and outcomes. Integral to the model are the adoption of culturally responsive evidence-based practices and interventions to support the achievement of academic and behavioural goals, objectives, and outcomes for all students. Implementation of the model rests on the formation of a school-wide team that oversees the efficient organisation of resources, as well as examining data for patterns of cultural disadvantage. Staff are supported by continuous practice-based professional learning and work to broaden and deepen their cultural perspectives to create structures and practices that consider the cultural needs of students in the learning process.

The model should be implemented and evaluated according to school needs, which makes it difficult to form an evidence base on MTCRSS, as the model is contextual. Like other multi-tiered systems of support, the interventions within the framework are evidence-based, but the frameworks themselves are not (Stoiber & Gettinger, 2015). The remainder of this volume will discuss a variety of at-risk groups of students and evidence-based approaches that can be used to support their success under the MTCRSS model.

References

Anderson, A. A. (2004). *Theory of change as a tool for strategic planning*. Washington, DC: The Aspen Institute. Retrieved from www.wallacefoundation.org/knowledge-center/Documents/Theory-of-Change-Tool-for-Strategic-Planning-Report-on-Early-Experiences.pdf

Banks, J. A. (2016). *Cultural diversity and education* (6th ed.). New York, NY: Routledge.

Barrett, S., Eber, L., & Weist, M. (Eds.). (2013). *Advancing education effectiveness: Interconnecting school mental health an school-wide positive behaviour support*. Retrieved from www.pbis.org/common/pbisresources/publications/Final-Monograph.pdf

Bianco, M., & Harris, B. (2016). Strength-based RTI. *Gifted Child Today, 37*(3), 169–176.

Blase, K., & Fixsen, D. (2013). *Core intervention components: Identifying and operationalizing what makes programs work*. ASPE Research Brief. Washington, DC: U.S Department of Health and Human Services.

Breakwell, G., Hammon, S., Fife-Schaw, C., & Smith, J. A. (Eds.). (2007). *Research methods in psychology* (3rd ed.). Thousand Oaks, CA: Sage Publications.

Bronfenbrenner, U. (1989). Ecological systems theory. *Annals of Child Development, 6*, 187–249.

Cooper, J. O., Heron, T. E., & Heward, W. L. (2013). *Applied behaviour analysis*. Upper Saddle River, NJ: Pearson Higher Education.

Creswell, J. W. (2009). *Research design: Qualitative, quantitative, and mixed methods approaches* (3rd ed.). Thousand Oaks, CA: Sage Publications.

De Nobile, J., Lyons, G., & Arthur-Kelly, M. (2017). *Positive learning environments: Creating and maintaining productive classrooms*. Melbourne, VIC, Australia: Cengage Learning.

CAST. (2011a). *About UDL*. Retrieved December 5, 2014 from www.cast.org/udl/index.html

CAST. (2011b). *Universal design for learning guidelines – version 2.0*. Wakefield, MA: Author. Retrieved March 10, 2014 from www.udlcenter.org/aboutudl/udlguidelines/downloads

Dix, K. L., Slee, P. T., Lawson, M. J., & Keeves, J. P. (2012). Implementation quality of whole-school mental health promotion and students' academic performance. *Child and Adolescent Mental Health, 17*, 45–51. doi:http://dx.doi.org/10.1111/j.1475-3588.2011.00608.x

Drame, E. R., & Xu, Y. (2008). Examining sociocultural factors in response to intervention models. *Childhood Education, 85*(4), 26–32.

Fogarty International Center. (2017). *Implementation science information and resources*. Retrieved from www.fic.nih.gov/researchtopics/pages/implementationscience.aspx

Fuchs, D., & Deshler, D. D. (2007). What we need to know about responsiveness to intervention (and shouldn't be afraid to ask). *Learning Disabilities Research & Practice, 22*(2), 129–136.

Gay, G. (2013). Teaching through and to cultural diversity. *The Ontario Institute for Studies in Education of the University of Toronto Curriculum Inquiry, 43*(1), 48–69.

Hmelo-Silver, C. E., & Barrows, H. S. (2006). Goals and strategies of a problem-based learning facilitator. *Interdisciplinary Journal of Problem-Based Learning, 1*, 21–39.

Jimerson, S., Burns, M., & VanDerHeyden, A. (2016). *Handbook of response to intervention* (2nd ed.). New York, NY: Springer Publishing.

John-Steiner, V., & Mahn, H. (1996). Sociocultural approaches to learning and development: A Vygotskian framework. *Educational Psychologist, 31*, 191–206.

Klinger, J. K., & Edwards, P. A. (2006). Cultural considerations with response to intervention models. *Reading Research Quarterly, 41*(1), 108–117.

Lane, K. L., Menzies, H. M., Ennis, R. P., & Bezdek, J. (2013). School-wide systems to promote positive behaviours and facilitate instruction. *Journal of Curriculum and Instruction, 7*(1), 6–31.

McIntosh, K., & Goodman, S. (2016). *Integrated multi-tiered systems of support: Blending RTI and PBIS*. New York, NY: Guilford Press.

Morales-James, C., Lopez, L., Wilkins, R., & Fergus, E. (n.d.). *Cultural adaptations when implementing RTI in urban settings: RTI action network*. Retrieved from www.rtinetwork.org/learn/diversity/cultural-adaptations-when-implementing-rti-in-urban-settings

National Association of School Psychologists. (2009). *Appropriate academic supports to meet the needs of all students* (Position Statement). Bethesda, MD: Author.

Office of Learning Supports at Colorado Department of Education. (2015). *What is MTSS?* Retrieved from www.cde.state.co.us/mtss/whatismtss

Organizational Research Services. (2004). *Theory of change: A practical tool for action, results, and learning*. Seattle, WA: Organizational Research Services. Retrieved from www.aecf.org/m/resourcedoc/aecf-theoryofchange-2004.pdf#page=6

OSEP Technical Assistance Center on Positive Behavioural Interventions and Supports. (2015, October). *Positive Behavioural Interventions and Supports (PBIS) implementation blueprint: Part 1 – foundations and supporting information*. Eugene, OR: University of Oregon. Retrieved from www.pbis.org

Papert, S., & Harel, I. (1991). Situating constructionism. In *Constructionism* (pp. 193–206). Ablex Publishing Corporation. Retrieved from www.papert.org/articles/SituatingConstructionism.html

Ridgeway, T. R., Price, D. P., Simpson, C. G., & Rose, C. A. (2011). Reviewing the roots of response to intervention: Is there enough research to support the promise? *Administrative Issues Journal: Education, Practice, and Research*, *2*(1), 85–95. doi:10.5929/2011.2.1.8

Sabelli, N. (2008). *Constructionism: A new opportunity for elementary science education* (pp. 193–206). DRL Division of Research on Learning in Formal and Informal Settings. Retrieved from http://nsf.gov/awardsearch/showAward.do?AwardNumber=8751190

Stoiber, K. C., & Gettinger, M. (2015). Multi-tiered systems of support and evidence-based practices. In S. R. Jimerson, M. K. Burns, & A. M. VanDerHeyden (Eds.), *Handbook of response to intervention* (pp. 121–141). New York, NY: Springer Publishing.

Sugai, G. (2017, March). *Operationalizing and integrating MTSS & prevention & behavioral sciences*. Paper presented at the 14th International Conference on Positive Behaviour Support, San Diego, CA.

Sugai, G., & Horner, R. H. (2009). Responsiveness-to-intervention and school-wide positive behavior supports: Integration of multi-tiered system approaches. *Exceptionality*, *17*(4), 223–237.

Talpin, D. H., & Clark, H. (2012). *Theory of change basics. A primer on theory of change*. New York, NY: Act Knowledge. Retrieved from www.theoryofchange.org/wp-content/uploads/toco_library/pdf/ToCBasics.pdf

Tomlinson, C. (2008). The goals of differentiation. *Educational Leadership*, *66*(3), 26–30.

University of Washington Center for Educational Leadership. (2015). *Creating a theory of action for improving teaching and learning*. Retrieved from http://info.k-12leadership.org/hs-fs/hub/381270/file-2166618739-pdf/documents/webinar-presentation-pdfs/creating-a-theory-of-action.pdf

Vavrus, M. (2008). Culturally responsive teaching. In T. L. Good (Ed.), *21st century education: A reference handbook* (vol. 2, pp. 49–57). Thousand Oaks, CA: Sage Publishing.

3

AT-RISK STUDENTS

English learners, migrant/refugee, and indigenous students

Introduction

Some students are more at-risk for school failure based on aspects of their background such as their language learning. Immigration due to economic or political circumstances results in classrooms with increasing numbers of students of migrant or refugee status. Language learning can also be an issue for students from indigenous backgrounds. Students from these groups tend to experience more significant impacts on their ability to access education, due to needing to learn the new, dominant language, transition stress/cultural shock, and often trauma. Educators need to fully understand how these impact learning and behaviour before they can understand how to best support these students. This chapter will describe who English language learners (ELLs) are and the impacts of having to learn language on top of other social-emotional issues. It will also outline practices within the multi-tiered culturally responsive system of support (MTCRSS) model that educators can incorporate in order to effectively support these students.

Language learners

As outlined previously, a new language may need to be learned to function both academically and behaviourally in the school context. In the following section, the different types of language learners will be defined and their challenges described.

English language learners (ELLs)

ELLs are simply defined as students who are in the process of developing their proficiency in English (Savignon, 1983). English learners are one of the fastest growing populations in schools in the English-speaking world. In the United States, approximately 5 million students are identified as ELLs and represent around 9% of the school population (National Center for Educational Statistics, 2017). Most ELLs in the US are native-born, from Spanish-speaking backgrounds (National Education Association, 2017). In Canada, the foreign-born population tripled between 1981 and 2011, with more than 200 languages reported as a home language (Statistics Canada, 2015). Although the school population in general has remained steady, the number of students enrolled in second language immersion programs has increased by 14% from 2000–2009, when about 317,000 students were enrolled in these programs (Statistics Canada, 2011). In the United Kingdom (UK), as of 2013, over one million students spoke a language other than English as their first language, coming from 360 different language groups (Arnot et al., 2014).

In other English-speaking countries with smaller populations, such as Australia, one-fifth of students are ELLs (O'Connor et al., 2017) and come from over 200 ethnic backgrounds (Australian Bureau of Statistics, 2016). In New Zealand, the introduction of a more open immigration policy in 1991 resulted in a dramatic increase in the number of ELLs in schools (Stacey, 2009). As of 2008, there were 165 different ethnic groups from 160 countries speaking 110 different languages in New Zealand schools (Stacey, 2009). There are approximately 29,000 students in almost 1,200 schools receiving ESOL funding for English language learning support (Stacey, 2009).

Because Canada is a bilingual country, with both English and French as official languages, in addition to second language programs aimed at Anglophone students, all provinces also offer minority language programs aimed at students whose native language is French in provinces other than Quebec and for those whose native language is English in Quebec (Statistics Canada, 2011).

Students who are ELLs can be impacted by factors that occur outside of school. ELLs live in poverty at higher rates than the general population and are two times as likely to be living in poverty (Skinner, Wight, Aratani, Cooper, & Thampi, 2010). This is often due to their parents/carers having to work in low paid, entry-level jobs due to limited English skills or the lack of recognition of their educational qualifications by their new country. Living in poverty reduces the educational opportunities that families can provide to their children and can impact their physical and mental health (Ferguson, Bovaird, & Mueller, 2007).

ELLs are particularly at-risk in the education system due to teachers' lack of awareness of how to distinguish issues associated with learning a language from those caused by trauma or underlying learning disabilities. Understanding how students learn English can reduce the number of ELLs who are inappropriately referred to special education or are not referred for special education or mental health evaluation because of the complexity of assessing students learning English (U.S. Department of Education, Office of English Language Acquisition, 2016). Educators need professional development so that they can appropriately assist teams in identifying and supporting the unique needs that ELLs present in academic settings (Nguyen, 2012).

Due to a lack of testing accommodations, ELLs often perform poorly in assessments, and particularly in high-stakes testing (National Education Association, 2017). This results in ELLs accounting for a high percentage of students performing at below grade level, leading to high dropout rates. This issue exists in the US but also other countries such as Australia.

Migrant children

It is acknowledged that the term "migrant child" may have different meanings in different countries. A migrant child is defined in the United States as:

> a child who is, or whose parent, spouse, or guardian is, a migratory agricultural worker, including a migratory dairy worker, or a migratory fisher, and who, in the preceding 36 months, in order to obtain, or accompany such parent, spouse, guardian in order to obtain, temporary or seasonal employment has moved from one school district to another.
>
> *(U.S. Department of Education, 2006; 34 CFR Part 200)*

Traditionally, students of migrant workers have been one of the most disadvantaged groups in United States schools (Cranston-Gingras & Paul, 2008).

Migrant children in the US, due to their frequent mobility and lack of opportunity to exert influence in their setting, are often called "invisible children". There are specific federal guidelines for qualifying as a migrant student in US schools. These guidelines are:

1 The child must be younger than 21 years old.
2 The child is entitled to free public education.
3 The child is a migratory agricultural worker or migratory fisher or the child has a parent, spouse or guardian who is a migratory work or fisher.
4 The child has moved within the previous 36 months in order for the family to find work (According to the regulations for Title I, Part C, Education of Migratory Children).

In 2014–2015, there were 332,335 migrant youth eligible for services in K-12 schools in the US (Glander, 2016). The number of migrant youth is likely much higher, as they are difficult to identify due to their constant mobility. Some characteristics of migrant students that place them at educational risk are frequent absences from school due to working with parents in the field or caring for younger siblings, and moving from school to school (Romanowski, 2003). Migrant students often start the school year late and leave early in order to follow the seasonal work patterns. Factors of migratory living put students at greater risk for becoming identified with a disability (Cranston-Gingras & Paul, 2008). These factors include: (a) low levels of parent education, (b) English language acquisition, (c) poor health care, (d) dangerous living conditions, and (e) extreme poverty (50% of migratory families live below the poverty line). Cranston-Gingras and Paul (2008) highlight that many migrant children in the US work with their families and may therefore be exposed to toxic pesticides, dangerous farm equipment, and poor sanitation at rates higher than that of other children. They also work long hours before and/or after school. These factors put migrant youth at risk for falling behind in school and dropping out.

Migrant children in other countries such as the UK and Australia are seen as the children of migrant parents who have legally migrated for work reasons (Hamilton, 2013a). Regardless of definition, these "children are the recipients of involuntary displacement" and experience a range of challenges (Hamilton, 2013a, p. 174). Migrant children in other English-speaking countries are believed to experience profound loss and challenges due to change of rules, roles, and routines at school and in the wider community (Hamilton, 2013a). Students who migrate to a new country with their families often need to acquire the language of their new country. Further, they can experience social isolation due to anxieties surrounding their lack of English and also experience the issues of ELLs in general mentioned earlier.

Like ELLs in general, migrant children are often over-referred for special education (Hamilton, 2013b). Further, low socioeconomic status (SES) and lack of school supports impact the development, capacity to learn, and behaviour of migrant students.

Refugee students

People are on the move globally in unprecedented numbers due to conflict, violence, and economic migration (Eurostat, 2016). Children, accompanied and unaccompanied, are arriving in Europe, the US, and other developed, high-income nations as refugees that have experienced great trauma (Menjivar & Perreira, 2017). Refugee children have been forced to leave their home country under extreme circumstances such as war, natural disaster, or political oppression, and often the journey to reach their final destination has been difficult (Menjivar & Perreira, 2017). They likely arrived in their new country with few belongings and unmet needs. Researchers have documented the negative impacts on both the social and psychological development of refugee children (Strekalova & Hoot, 2008). On arrival, refugee children often experience barriers such as racism, marginalisation, and educational disadvantage due to lengthy stays in refugee camps (Devere, McDermott, & Verbitsky, 2006). It is common for refugees to live in refugee camps for 5–10 years, and of course this has a detrimental effect on students' educational development and outcomes (Oh & Van der Stouwe, 2008).

Specific educational policies regarding refugee students rarely exist; if these students are mentioned in policy at all they are combined with other categories such as ELL students (Arnot & Pinson, 2005; Sidhu & Taylor, 2007). Arnot and Pinson (2005) identified three main areas where refugee students typically require support: learning, social, and emotional. They found that schools usually focus on ELL issues or emotional problems, with less attention being paid to supporting these students in accessing the mainstream curriculum. Less attention was given to other learning needs of the students, such as facilitating their access to the mainstream curriculum. The fact that many refugee students have experienced trauma may make it difficult to assess their strengths and needs (Rutter, 2006). Children from a refugee background may not have had the benefit of school, so are not literate in their own language and have an even harder time learning English.

Indigenous students

Indigenous students (also known as first peoples, aboriginal peoples, native peoples, or autochthonous peoples) are students who are descended from and identify with the original inhabitants of a given region. Students who are indigenous are impacted by higher rates of poverty, drug and alcohol abuse, suicide, and poor health outcomes (Friesen & Krauth, 2010), which may impact their progress in schools. Indigenous students typically do not make the same educational progress as their non-indigenous peers. This may be due to the discrepancy between indigenous cultures and the dominant Western culture. Another repercussion of this cultural mismatch in education may be that of lower teacher expectations of this group of students. This may have a negative effect on student learning, as many indigenous students are tracked into life skills or vocational programs because of these lower teacher expectations, and this can negatively affect student academic outcomes (Castagno & Brayboy, 2008). Governments have responded to the problem of negative outcomes with educational initiatives.

The Australian government has committed to "closing the gap" and improving outcomes for indigenous Australians through policy and programs. They have created several targets for indigenous students: (a) increasing participation in early childhood education, (b) improving school attendance, (c) improving reading, writing, and numeracy, and (d) improving school retention (Australian Government, Department of Education and Training, 2017). In addition to creating targets, the government has released a funding package to support the implementation of practices to help schools meet the targets.

In New Zealand, where many of the non-English speaking students are from indigenous and Pacific Islander groups, full immersion (in Te Reo Mäori and Pasifika languages) and bilingual English programs are available. There were 2,581 schools with 760,859 children attending in New Zealand as of July 2009, and over 3,500 of these students were enrolled in these programs (New Zealand Ministry of Education, 2009).

Teachers typically have limited awareness of their indigenous students' language backgrounds, particularly of contact language varieties, and little understanding of effective educational responses (McTaggart & Curro, 2009). While language awareness has been found to provide a necessary conceptual basis for acknowledging contact languages, additional understandings and capacities have been identified as essential for effective classroom responses. These include an understanding of multilingualism and second language acquisition, an ability to analyse the language demands of curriculum content, and the ability to plan for and teach the language in which this content is delivered.

Second language acquisition

Several theories exist to explain how people acquire a second language (Chomsky, 1957; Cummins, 1981; Krashen, 1987; Skinner, 1968). These theories are greatly influenced by first language acquisition theories. These theories attempt to explain how EL learners are acquiring English while in the school setting. These theories can also be used to determine effective programming for EL learners.

Behaviourist theory

Behaviourist theory of language acquisition dominated the field from the 1940s to the 1960s. Much of behaviour theory was based on the work of B. F. Skinner. Skinner (1968) extended his conditional learning theory to incorporate language. He believed language learning was very similar to other types of learning. Behaviour theorists believed that language learning (first or second) was learned through two processes, imitation and repetitive action (Macaro, 2003). They believed that language is learned through a series of mechanisms, including the development of new language habits. Behaviourists also believe that first language habits may be impediments to learning the habits of the second language, because second language learners must replace the habits of their primary language with the habits of their second language (Gass & Selinker, 2001).

Behaviourists believe second language acquisition is explained through imitation, repetition, and reinforcement of syntax and morphology. They also posit that learners learn phrases similar to their first language more easily. Phrases that vary greatly from a learner's first language will require much more practice for learning (Macaro, 2003). The behaviourist theory of language acquisition states that children learn language through a stimulus, response, and reinforcement cycle. Children are exposed to language from the environment, produce a response to the environment, and learn from the reinforcement to their response (Peregoy & Boyle, 2013). Therefore, phrases that are similar to the primary language require little stimulus, response, and reinforcement, while phrases that are very different from the primary language require many cycles of stimulus, response, and reinforcement.

However, behaviourist theory does not explain all of the events seen in children acquiring two languages. One major criticism of this theory is that it does not explain phrases that children speak that are not imitations of adults (e.g., two mouses). Linguists such as Chomsky began to notice that children did not speak in the large phrases that were memorised. Chomsky theorised that because children are able to use the words they know and make new sentences, they must have an internal device for learning language. Chomsky (1957) became a leader in the innatist theory of second language acquisition.

Innatist theory

Innatists believe that children are born with a certain capacity for learning language, because humans are genetically built to learn and convey language. Chomsky (1957) believed that the human brain has a mechanism for language, the language acquisition device (LAD). The LAD is pre-programmed to infer the rules of language when it is stimulated by language. Once the LAD has been turned on, children begin to discover the patterns of language and internalise grammar rules. Innatists believe that language is acquired and not learned (White Soltero, 2004).

Chomsky's theory of first language acquisition had an impact on the theories of second language acquisition. One theory that developed from Chomsky's work was Dulay, Burt, and Krashen's (1987) creative construction theory. This theory is based on the premise that EL learners make similar mistakes while learning English that their monolingual English peers make. When they are developing English language skills, EL learners construct the same rules for second language acquisition that are observed in English first language acquisition. An example of this would be children who overgeneralise the -s ending rules to words that are exceptions (e.g., mans for men). Continuing the innatist theory development, Krashen developed his own theory of second language acquisition. Krashen's theory of second-language acquisition (1987, 1988) consists of five hypotheses: (a) acquisition-learning hypothesis, (b) monitor hypothesis, (c) natural order hypothesis, (d) input hypothesis, and (e) affective filter hypothesis.

Interactionist theory

Interactionists believe that language is learned through a stimulus, response, and reinforcement pattern and that humans are born with an ability to learn language. Language is produced by genetic and environmental factors. In this theory, family or caregivers are a critical piece in the child's language acquisition, as they facilitate the child's ability to use their innate language (Peregoy & Boyle, 2013). Interactionists believe that language acquisition occurs from communication and that acquisition is facilitated by caregivers. They also believe that the child's innate ability and the environment both play an important piece in the child's ability to learn language. Children will make greater progress in a language if they have opportunities to interact with native speakers of the language (Peregoy & Boyle, 2013).

Interactionists also believe that during the process of second language acquisition, interaction between native and non-native speakers is central to acquisition. These natural conversations provide opportunities to non-native speakers to express themselves and therefore be exposed to more comprehensible input as they learn the language. When EL learners are in a natural setting, they will use language that they understand and interact with others who speak at a level higher than their own.

Common underlying proficiency theory

Cummins (1981) developed the common underlying proficiency theory, the most widely applied theory of second-language acquisition. This theory incorporates both psychological and cognitive factors in the language acquisition process. Specifically, Cummins (1981) hypothesised a developmental interdependence influenced by the importance of cognitive skills in the language process. He contended that there is a direct correlation between a person's first language acquisition and competency and their second-language development. In other words, they use the same cognitive skills to acquire their first language in the acquisition of the second language. This theory of second-language acquisition comprises two components, basic interpersonal communication skills (BICS) and cognitive/academic language proficiency (CALP).

Basic interpersonal communication skills (BICS) involve the informal language of conversation. Children typically learn BICS through informal interaction with their peers, often while playing. Acquiring this level of communication skill takes between two and three years of coverage to the target language. Children with good BICS will be able to discuss topics with which they are very familiar (e.g. school, television programs). Cognitive academic language proficiency is language skills associated with literacy and cognitive development. As opposed to BICS, these skills are learned most often through formal instruction in school. Cognitive academic language is typically learned at school, so it takes much longer to develop. According to Cummins (1991), it takes a learner 5–10 years to obtain CALP. This is the type of language that is necessary to learn in the content areas.

In summary, current theories of second language acquisition centre around genetic ability and environment. The behaviourist theory of language acquisition states that children learn language through a stimulus, response, and reinforcement cycle. Innatists believe that children are born with a certain capacity for learning language. Interactionists believe that language is learned through a stimulus, response, and reinforcement pattern and that humans are born with an ability to learn language. One of the most popular interactionist theories is the common underlying proficiency theory, which incorporates BICS and CALP and describes the time that is necessary for a child to be able to learn and learn from a language. Understanding these theories is vital when discussing educational models that are used to educate EL learners.

Supporting students in a multi-tiered culturally responsive system of support

Students who are migrant, refugee, learning English and/or indigenous have needs that are often unmet in the educational setting. For example, indigenous culture focuses on the community as a whole, so learning is connected to communal well-being. Learning often occurs through storytelling, with legends used to transmit social values such as humility, honesty, courage, and respect. In order to effectively support these students, educators need to meet these needs through carefully planning all tiers of the MTCRSS model. In order to fully support these groups of students through the MTCRSS model, there needs to be additional considerations when preparing for the education of all students. These considerations include:

- ELLs' learning processes
- Trauma-informed practice
- Mismatches between cultural beliefs and Western culture/school beliefs

Rutter (2006) has identified three components of best practice for these vulnerable populations: a welcoming environment, free of racism; the need to meet social and emotional needs, particularly for students who have experienced trauma; and linguistic needs. Rutter also emphasised that successful interventions viewed children holistically, working to meet both academic and social-behavioural learning needs. These suggestions are well aligned with the five tenets of cultural responsiveness integrated into the current model: (a) empowerment, (b) equity pedagogy, (c) prejudice reduction, (d) knowledge construction, and (e) content integration.

Tier 1: (universal) supports

As Tier 1 is focused on universal supports for all students, schools can implement several evidence-based practices to promote an empowering school culture that reduces prejudice, includes all students, and is safe. Student clubs can allow students to maintain their cultural identity (indigenous student society) while promoting a feeling of belonging and *reducing prejudice* by exposing students to a diversity of cultures (Khan & Reis, 2006). The creation of mentor programs that are culturally sensitive can serve the same purposes. *Content integration* can be implemented school-wide by ensuring that the school library has an equitable number of culturally relevant books and resources and that the textbooks chosen for classrooms are also culturally relevant.

In Tier 1 of the MTCRSS model, the primary focus is on high-quality research-based instruction (Esparza Brown & Sanford, 2011). In order to support the students described in this chapter, their additional needs that need to be met through the MTCRSS model must be fully understood when choosing the Tier 1 general education curriculum. The majority of educational research centres on the needs of monolingual English-speaking students. Because of this, educators need to be vigilant to ensure that the general education curriculum adopted will meet the language and diversity needs of English language learners, migrant youth, indigenous students, and refugee children to ensure that *knowledge construction is taking place.* Curricular *content* should reflect the population of students by *integrating* their histories, language, and customs. The basis of MTCRSS is being able to make evidence-based instructional decisions for students. Therefore, the context of the research that has been done as the basis for the chosen curriculum must be fully understood.

Schools should provide continual professional development about the needs of these groups to the faculty and staff of the school setting. Ongoing and research-based professional development around the issues of oral language development, literacy, students' primary and/or home language, contextual considerations, and the cultural background of students. This will *reduce prejudice*, allow for educators to make better-informed decisions, more correctly interpret screening and assessment results, and design appropriate interventions for students who require Tier 2 supports.

As students in these populations may have impacts on their language development through second language acquisition or missing large amounts of schooling, it is important that schools have high-quality, scaffolded language development included throughout the school day (Peregoy & Boyle, 2013). Educators can take a universal design to learning (UDL) approach to promote an *equity pedagogy* by scaffolding language and provide many opportunities for students to respond and use their English language (National Center on Universal Design for Learning, 2011). This will go a long way to making students feel *empowered* about their learning. Some examples of scaffolding language include paraphrasing key words, providing opportunities for students to expand their answers, supporting language by using synonyms and antonyms, rephrasing and repeating back students' responses, identify for students the correct aspects of the answer, and provide language supports Gargiulo and Metcalf (2017). Schools should provide direct instruction in English language development for students in these groups in Tier 1. This instruction should include oral language and vocabulary instruction which is provided to students using an evidenced-based curriculum. An additional concern educators will need to consider for students in these populations is the most appropriate language of instruction. Districts need to fully understand when students should be receiving bilingual instruction, as students' needs in this area will vary.

As Tier 1 requires that schools are conducting frequent assessment with all of the students in their schools, the school will need to ensure that the assessments being used are valid for progress monitoring data with these students. Students in these groups should be screened as often (at least three times a year) and should also be screened on the same indicators as the other students. The universal screenings should be conducted in the students' primary language, as well as English, and use measures that have high reliability and validity (National Center on Universal Design for Learning, 2011).

An important piece of Tier 1 is awareness of the social-emotional needs of all students in the school. Students in the groups described in this chapter may have needs that can be addressed in Tier 1. This prevention (Tier 1) approach to include trauma-informed skills/instruction should be linked to the basic general education behavioural curriculum (e.g. "respect, responsibility, safety expectations") and behavioural expectations (Rutter, 2006). When teaching the behavioural norms of the school, educators need to be aware of cultural mismatch which can occur. Ensuring that schools promote mental health wellness and positive life skills can prevent or reduce mental health concerns or problems from developing.

At all times, school should be experienced as a safe place for all students, one that is trauma-sensitive and has *empowering culture*. One way to ensure that all students perceive school as a safe place is through them feeling as if they belong (Cumming, Marsh, & Higgins, 2018). School needs to have predictable and consistent structures, routines, and rules for all students. This consistency will contribute to all students understanding behavioural expectations and consequences, which will allow for students to experience lower anxiety in the school setting. The understanding of the expectations and consequence will also allow students to have meaningful relationships with the adults on the campus, as their behaviour is predictable (Cumming et al., 2018).

Another way for students to have higher engagement with a school is through familial involvement. If the family perceives the school in a positive way, the students will also. Parent liaisons can work with families and encourage them to become involved in the school community (Khan & Reis, 2006). They can also provide home visits to the students' families to make them feel more welcomed. Communication from the school to the home, whether by phone, email, or written notice, should be provided in a language that is understood by the families. Telephone trees in multiple languages can assist in this regard. Parent conferences can be held off-campus in places that are closer to parents' and students' homes. Block parent meetings can be held several times a year for families who cannot attend school events because they live too far from school and lack transportation. The aim of these meetings is to address parent concerns and offer an opportunity to share school-related information. These meetings take place every two or three months in a community centre or nearby library.

The social-emotional needs of students should be monitored with the same frequency during the year as the academic monitoring. The progress monitoring is important for both social-emotional and academic needs to determine if students need to be supported through Tier 2 systems.

Tier 2: secondary prevention for some

Regardless of the level of English language proficiency or acculturation, students who are identified as still being at risk academically and/or behaviourally despite Tier 1 universal supports should be provided with evidence-based intervention in Tier 2. When students from these groups are identified as needing Tier 2 interventions, the problem-solving team needs to ensure that the additional needs of the students are met. Students in this tier need to be provided with multiple opportunities to participate in culturally relevant peer learning and small group instruction. This will allow them to have opportunities for *knowledge construction* by using oral language and sufficient intensity to support them in making progress towards their academic outcomes.

An additional concern is that students from these groups may be experiencing trauma. For students who are identified as having social-emotional difficulties that are not fully addressed by Tier 1 supports, they should be referred for assessment and further social-emotional support in Tier 2. It is important for teams to understand that students may have experienced trauma in some form (e.g., refugee from war torn country, frequent moves due to migrant status). Trauma-informed processes need to be a part of Tier 2 to meet the extra needs that students in these groups may present (Rutter, 2006). Students in this tier may participate in group interventions which promote social-emotional well-being and emotional regulation. When implemented in a culturally responsive way using *equity pedagogy*, social skills groups can be effective ways to promote appropriate social behaviours, *knowledge construction, prejudice reduction*, and healthy relationships. In Tier 2, social-emotional skills should continue to be progress monitored. Some examples of assessments include mood and feeling questionnaires, anxiety scales and depression inventories. These assessments should be culturally relevant and build off of Tier 1 assessments to continue to monitor student progress.

Tier 3: tertiary prevention for a few

Before considering a student for Tier 3, or special education, the team must determine whether the student's academic difficulties more likely reflect a disability than limited English proficiency or cultural mismatch. It is also important to take the student's Response to Interventions provided in the previous tiers into consideration. The student's progress must be compared to other students with similar language and/or cultural backgrounds. Students who are experiencing academic difficulty solely due to language proficiency cannot be identified as having a disability. The school decision-making team needs to consider all of the exclusionary factors before identifying a student for special education.

If a student is found to be eligible for special education services, an individualised education program (IEP) will be created. The IEP should include a summary of the student's strengths and areas where support is necessary. The student's background and culture are considered when determining what evidence-based interventions will be used to support him or her. All five tenets of cultural responsiveness should be present in this tier, as in the others. For example, teachers should be using *equity pedagogy* and materials where the student's culture is *integrated into the content.*

Students in these groups who are experiencing behavioural or social-emotional difficulties will receive individualised, intensive supports, which may include functional behavioural assessment, a behavioural intervention plan, individual counselling, and maybe a referral to a mental health professional. It is crucial that students and families have a voice in the planning and implementation of supports at this tier, to promote self-determination skills and *empowerment.*

Conclusion

The increased movement of people globally has translated into classrooms that are becoming increasingly diverse, requiring educators to have an increased awareness of the cultural and linguistic issues that face some students, which are often compounded by exposure to trauma. These issues need to be addressed in order to effectively support this population of students academically and social-emotionally. The MTCRSS model is an effective solution to providing support for English language learners and migrant and refugee students as well as indigenous students.

References

Arnot, M., & Pinson, H. (2005). *The education of asylum-seeker and refugee children: A study of LEA and school values, policies and practices*. Cambridge: Faculty of Education, University of Cambridge.

Arnot, M., Schneider, C., Evans, M., Liu, Y., Welply, O., & Davies-Tutt, D. (2014). *School approaches to the education of EAL students*. Cambridge: The Bell Foundation.

Australian Bureau of Statistics. (2016). *2016 census*. Retrieved from www.abs.gov.au/websitedbs/censushome.nsf/home/2016

Australian Government Department of Education and Training. (2017). *Indigenous education*. Retrieved from www.education.gov.au/indigenous-schooling

Castagno, A., & Brayboy, B. (2008). Culturally responsive schooling for indigenous youth: A review of the literature. *Review of Educational Research, 78*, 941–993. doi:10.3102/0034654308323036

Chomsky, N. (1957). *Syntactic structures*. The Hague: Mouton.

Cranston-Gingras, A., & Paul, J. L. (2008). Ethics and students with disabilities from migrant farm worker families. *Rural Special Education Quarterly, 27*(1/2), 24–29.

Cumming, T., Marsh, R., & Higgins, K. (2018). *School connectedness for students with disabilities: From theory to evidence-based practice*. Melbourne, VIC, Australia: Routledge.

Cummins, J. (1981). The role of primary language development in promoting educational success for language minority students. In California Department of Education (Ed.), *School and language minority students: A theoretical framework* (pp. 3–50). Los Angeles, CA: Evaluation, Dissemination, and Assessment Center.

Cummins, J. (1991). Interdependence of first-and second-language proficiency in bilingual children. In E. Bialystok (Ed.), *Language processing in bilingual children* (pp. 70–89). Cambridge: Cambridge University Press.

Devere, H., McDermott, K., & Verbitsky, J. (2006). Just a refugee: Rights and status of refugees in New Zealand. In F. Crepeau et al. (Eds.), *Forced migration and global processes* (pp. 343–367). Lanham, Boulder: Lexington Books.

Dulay, H. C., Burt, M. K., & Krashen, S. D. (1987). *Language two*. Oxford: Oxford University Press.

Ervin-Tripp, S. M. (1974). Is second language learning like the first? *TESOL Quarterly, 8*(2), 111–127.

Esparza Brown, J., & Sanford, A. (2011). *RTI for English language learners: Appropriately using screening and progress monitoring tools to improve instructional outcomes*. Washington, DC: U.S. Department of Education, Office of Special Education Programs, National Center on Response to Intervention. Retrieved from www.rti4success.org/images/stories/pdfs/rtiforells.pdf

Eurostat. (2016). *Asylum applicants considered to be unaccompanied minors – annual data*. Retrieved November 28, 2016, from http://ec.europa.eu/eurostat/web/products-datasets/-/tps00194

Ferguson, H. B., Bovaird, S., & Mueller, M. P. (2007). The impact of poverty on educational outcomes for children. *Paediatrics Child Health, 12*, 701–706.

Friesen, J., & Krauth, B. (2010). *Sorting, peers and achievement of aboriginal students in British Columbia*. Working Paper, Centre for Education Research and Policy, Simon Fraser University. Retrieved from www.csls.ca/events/cea2009/friesen-krauth.pdf

Gargiulo, R. M., & Metcalf, D. (2017). *Teaching in today's inclusive classrooms: A universal design for learning approach*. Chicago: Cengage Learning.

Gass, S. M., & Selinker, L. (2001). *Second language acquisition: An introductory* course. Mahwah, NJ: Lawrence Erlbaum Associates.

Glander, M. (2016). *Selected statistics from the public elementary and secondary education universe: School year 2014–2015* (NCES 2016–2076). U.S. Department of Education. Washington, DC: National Center for Education Statistics. Retrieved from http://nces.ed.gov/pubsearch

Hamilton, P. L. (2013a). It's not all about academic achievement: Supporting the social and emotional needs of migrant worker children. *Pastoral Care in Education, 31*, 173–190. doi:10.1080/02643944.2012.747555

Hamilton, P. L. (2013b). Including migrant worker children in the learning and social context of the rural primary school. *Education, 41*, 202–217. doi:10.1080/03004279.2011.569737

Khan, C., & Reis, J. (2006). *Promoting youth development through school-based group mentoring: An evaluation study of TALKS mentoring*. Retrieved May 22, 2017, from www.talksmentoring.org/research.htm

Krashen, S. (1987). *Principles and practice in second language acquisition*. New York, NY: Prentice Hall International.

Krashen, S. (1988). *Second language acquisition and second language learning*. New York, NY: Prentice Hall International.

Macaro, E. (2003). *Teaching and learning a second language: A guide to recent research and its applications*. London: Continuum.

McTaggart, R., & Curro, G. (2009). *Book language as a foreign language – ESL strategies for indigenous learners*. Report. Toowong, QLD: Queensland College of Teachers.

Menjivar, C., & Perreira, K. M. (2017). Undocumented and unaccompanied: Children of migration in the European Union and the United States. *Journal of Ethic and Migration Studies*, Online first, 1–21. doi:10.1080/1369183X.2017.1404255

National Center for Educational Statistics. (2017). *English language learners in public schools*. Retrieved from https://nces.ed.gov/programs/coe/indicator_cgf.asp

National Center on Universal Design for Learning. (2011). *FAQs from the national UDL task force*. Retrieved from www.udlcenter.org/advocacy/faq_guides/ell

National Education Association. (2017). *English language learners*. Retrieved from www.nea.org/home/32346.htm

New Zealand Ministry of Education. (2009). *Education statistics of New Zealand 2009*. Retrieved from www.educationcounts.govt.nz/__data/assets/pdf_file/0017/80225/2009-Education-Statistics-of-NZ-Booklet.pdf

Nguyen, H. T. (2012). Education teachers collaborate to support English language learners with learning disabilities. *Issues in Teacher Education, 21*, 127–152.

O'Connor, M., O'Connor, E., Tarasuik, J., Gray, S., Kvalsig, A., & Goldfield, S. (2017). Academic outcomes of multilingual children in Australia. *International Journal of Speech-Language Pathology*, Online first, 1–13. doi:10.1080/17549507.2017.1292546

Oh, S. A., & van der Stouwe, M. (2008). Education, diversity, and inclusion in Burmese refugee camps in Thailand. *Comparative Education Review, 52*(4), 589–617.

Peregoy, O., & Boyle, S. (2013). *Reading, writing, and learning in ESL: A resource book for K-12 teachers* (7th ed.). Boston: Pearson Education, Inc.

Romanowski, M. H. (2003). Meeting the unique needs of the children of migrant farm workers. *The Clearing House: A Journal of Educational Strategies, Issues and Ideas*, 77(1), 27–33.

Rutter, J. (2006). *Refugee children in the UK*. Maidenhead, Berkshire: Open University Press.

Savignon, S. J. (1983). *Communicative competence: Theory and classroom practice*. Reading, MA: Addison-Wesley.

Sidhu, R., & Taylor, S. (2007). Educational provision for refugee youth in Australia: Left to chance? *Journal of Sociology, 43*(3), 283–300.

Skinner, B. F. (1968). *The technology of teaching*. New York, NY: Appleton-Century-Crofts.

Skinner, C., Wight, V. R., Aratani, Y., Cooper, J. L., & Thampi, K. (2010). *English language proficiency, family economic security, and child development*. National Center for Children in Poverty. Retrieved March 27, 2018, from www.nccp.org/publications/pdf/text_948.pdf

Stacey, K. (2009). Professional development for bilingual tutors in New Zealand: A pedagogy of support. *TESOL in Context, S2*. Retrieved from www.tesol.org.au/files/files/100_Stacey.pdf

Statistics Canada. (2011). *Public school indicators for Canada, the provinces and territories, 2000/2001 to 2008/2009*. Retrieved from www.statcan.gc.ca/pub/81-004-x/2011001/article/11433-eng.htm

Statistics Canada. (2015). *Linguistic characteristics of Canadians*. Retrieved from www12.statcan.gc.ca/census-recensement/2011/as-sa/98-314-x/98-314-x2011001-eng.cfm

Strekalova, E., & Hoot, J. (2008). What is special about special needs of refugee children? Guidelines for teachers. *Multicultural Education*, 21–24.

U.S. Department of Education. (2006). *Title I – improving the academic achievement of the disadvantaged*. 34 C.F. R. § 200.81(d).

U.S. Department of Education, Office of English Language Acquisition. (2016). *English learner tool kit for State and Local Education Agencies (SEAs and LEAs)*. Washington, DC: Author.

White Soltero, S. (2004). *Dual language: Teaching and learning in two languages*. Boston: Pearson Education, Inc.

4

AT-RISK STUDENTS

Students with disabilities, mental health issues, and chronic illness

Introduction

Today's schools are becoming increasingly diverse, and more students than ever are considered to be at-risk for academic failure and poor post-school outcomes. Each student is an individual, with their own individual culture, strengths, and needs. Some of these groups of students are formally identified, and often schools receive funding earmarked to support students with disabilities, mental health issues, and chronic illness. Each of these are examined in terms of the impact they may have on a child's schooling in terms of the types of support needed for successful outcomes. Evidence-based practices and how they can be implemented within a multi-tiered culturally responsive system of support (MTCRSS) are proposed.

Students with disabilities

Students with disabilities comprise 7% of all school children in Australia (ABS, 2014) 8.5% in the UK (GOV.UK, 2014) and 13% in the US (NCES, 2017). The disparity in percentages may be due to how disability is defined, funded, and supported in each country. The US has prescriptive legislation, the Individuals with Disabilities Education Act of 2004, that mandates methods of identification and service provision of students with disabilities, while disability education legislation in Australia, Disability Standards for Education, and the UK, Children and Families Act 2014, are broader, leaving its interpretation and operationalisation to local education authorities.

The very definition of disabilities varies considerably. As there is no agreed upon definition, the United Nations (2006) definition in Article 1 of the *UN Convention on Rights of Persons with Disabilities* will be used throughout this volume:

> Persons with disabilities include those who have long-term physical, mental, intellectual or sensory impairments which in interaction with various barriers may hinder their full and effective participation in society on an equal basis with others.

Disability categories may also vary, but generally comprise the following for school-age children: specific learning disability, speech or language impairment other health impairment, autism, intellectual disability, developmental disability, emotional disturbance, multiple disabilities, hearing impairment, or orthopaedic impairment (NCES, 2017). The Australian Disability Standards for Education offer the following definition of disability:

> Disability, in relation to a person, means:
>
> (a) total or partial loss of the person's bodily or mental functions; or
> (b) total or partial loss of a part of the body; or
> (c) the presence in the body of organisms causing disease or illness; or
> (d) the presence in the body of organisms capable of causing disease or illness; or
> (e) the malfunction, malformation or disfigurement of a part of the person's body; or
> (f) a disorder or malfunction that results in the person learning differently from a person without the disorder or malfunction; or
> (g) a disorder, illness or disease that affects a person's thought processes, perception of reality, emotions or judgement or that results in disturbed behaviour

The Standards do not conceptualise disability categorically; however, the Nationally Consistent Collection of Data on School Students with Disability uses that definition to provide categories for reporting on support services students with disabilities: physical, cognitive, sensory, and social-emotional. In the UK, students with disabilities are given the broad classification as having "special education needs" (SEN). GOV.UK (2017) provides the following examples of areas of need: "behaviour or ability to socialise, for example they struggle to make friends; reading and writing, for example because they have dyslexia; ability to understand things; concentration levels, for example because they have ADHD, and physical ability" (p. 1). See Table 4.1 for a comparison of categories across countries. The UK does not make sensory disabilities a special category, so it would seem that children with sensory support needs would receive support under the physical needs category. The fact that autism can conceivably fit into up to three of the Australian broad categories, depending on the support needs of individual children, demonstrates the importance of supporting the individual child, not a disability category.

Amid all of the disagreement around definition and terminology, there is agreement in how to support students with disabilities. First and foremost, each student

TABLE 4.1 Comparison of disability reporting categories across countries

Country	*Australia*	*United Kingdom*	*United States*
Source	Nationally Consistent Collection of Data on School Students with Disability	GOV.UK	National Center for Education Statistics
Disability categories	Physical disability	Physical ability Concentration levels	Other health impairment Orthopaedic impairment
	Cognitive disability	Reading and writing Ability to understand things	Autism Intellectual disability Developmental disability Specific learning disability
	Sensory disability		Speech or language impairment Autism Hearing impairment Visual impairment
	Social-emotional disability	Behaviour or ability to socialise	Emotional disturbance Autism

is assessed to determine his or her strengths and educational support needs (Henley, Ramsey, & Algozzine, 2008). This assessment should be holistic, covering physical, cognitive, and social-emotional domains (Henley et al., 2008). The data from these assessments are then used to develop an individual education program (IEP), which is sometimes known as a personalised learning plan (PLP) or an individual learning plan (ILP). These plans typically contain the student's strengths, present levels of functioning, and educational goals. The plan then provides a detailed account of the services and supports the student needs to achieve those goals, as well as accommodations and modifications that will be made to support the student. All three of the countries mentioned here have policies that either require or recommend the use of person- and family-centred planning, with the student and family having a voice in the educational planning process.

Students with mental health issues

Although childhood mental illness is often labelled as emotional and/or behavioural disabilities for the purposes of school, the authors recognise the unique support needs of this population and will examine the characteristics and support needs of students with mental health issues separately from those of students with disabilities. Lawrence et al. (2015) conducted a large-scale survey of the mental health of children and young people in Australia, resulting in a comprehensive report that presents a comprehensive picture of the mental health of young Australians. They found that one in seven children and adolescents experience mental health issues and that this number is comparable to international studies. Attention deficit/hyperactivity disorder (ADHD) was the most common mental disorder in children and adolescents, followed by anxiety disorders, major depressive disorder, and conduct disorder.

Attention deficit/hyperactivity disorder

ADHD is defined as: "A persistent pattern of inattention and/or hyperactivity-impulsivity that interferes with functioning or development" (APA, 2013, pp. 59–60). Children must have six or more symptoms and adolescents five or more symptoms (see Table 4.2) that persist for six months and directly impact on social and academic activities. ADHD can present as predominantly inattentive, predominantly hyperactive/impulsive, or a combination of the two, and can be classified as mild, moderate, or severe, depending on how many symptoms are present and how they affect functioning.

Anxiety disorders

Anxiety disorders include: social phobia, separation anxiety disorder, generalised anxiety disorder, and obsessive compulsive disorder (Lawrence et al., 2015).

TABLE 4.2 DSM-5 diagnostic criteria for ADHD: symptoms of inattention, hyperactivity, and impulsivity

Symptoms of inattention	*Symptoms of hyperactivity and impulsivity*
Often fails to give close attention to detail or makes mistakes	Often fidgets with or taps hands and feet, or squirms in seat
Often has difficulty sustaining attention in tasks or activities	Often leaves seat in situations when remaining seated is expected
Often does not seem to listen when spoken to directly	Often runs and climbs in situations where it is inappropriate (in adolescents or adults, may be limited to feeling restless)
Often does not follow through on instructions and fails to finish schoolwork or workplace duties	Often unable to play or engage in leisure activities quietly
Often has difficulty organising tasks and activities	Is often "on the go", acting as if "driven by a motor"
Often avoids, dislikes or is reluctant to engage in tasks that require sustained mental effort	Often talks excessively
Often loses things necessary for tasks or activities	Often blurts out answers before a question has been completed
Is easily distracted by extraneous stimuli	Often has difficulty waiting their turn
Is often forgetful in daily activities	Often interrupts or intrudes on others

Source: Reproduced with permission from American Psychiatric Association (2013)

Children who have social phobia typically have an intense fear of social and performance situations, such as speaking in class or starting a conversation with a peer (ADAA, 2016). Separation anxiety disorder is diagnosed when an older child (aged 7–9) is unable to leave a parent or family member and is difficult to calm after the family member leaves. This is more intense than the separation anxiety that typically occurs between the ages of 18 months and 3 years. Children with separation anxiety disorder my experience extreme homesickness and misery over being away from loved ones.

Generalised anxiety disorders are characterised by excessive worry about many things such as grades, peer relationships, and family issues (ADAA, 2016). Students with GAD may be perfectionists, and teachers may observe these students being hard on themselves and seeking constant approval or reassurance. Children and adolescents with obsessive compulsive disorders (OCD) characteristically experience unwanted and intrusive thoughts and feel compelled to repeatedly perform rituals and routines to ease anxiety (ADAA, 2016). OCD is typically diagnosed around age 10. In a classroom, students with OCD may have difficulty beginning or finishing tasks.

Major depressive disorder

Major depression is diagnosed when there are a number of symptoms present that interfere with the ability to sleep, study, eat, and enjoy activities that were once pleasurable. In children and adolescents, major depression may manifest itself by the child pretending to be sick, refusing to go to school, clinginess, sulking, misbehaviour, and/or irritability. Early identification of childhood depression is crucial, as if untreated, it often persists into adulthood (Psychology Today, 2017).

Before puberty, the disorder is equally prevalent in boys and girls, but by age 15, girls are twice as likely as boys to have experienced depression (March et al., 2004). Adolescence is a time of transition for most teens, and they are coping with many issues such as their personal identities, sexuality, gender issues, and independence. There is associated comorbidity of anxiety, disruptive behaviour, eating disorders, or substance abuse. Symptoms may include: (a) vague physical complaints such as headaches, muscle aches, stomach aches, or tiredness, (b) frequent absenteeism, (c) elopement, (d) outbursts of shouting, anger, or crying, (d) boredom, (e) loss of interest in playing and friends, (f) alcohol or substance misuse, (g) poor communication, (h) fear of death, and (i) reckless behaviour (APA, 2013). Teachers should have an awareness of these symptoms in order to assist in recognising students who may need additional support.

Conduct disorder

The APA (2013) DSM-5 Diagnostic Criteria for conduct disorders is as follows:

> A repetitive and persistent pattern of behaviour in which the basic rights of others or major age- appropriate societal norms or rules are violated, as

manifested by the presence of at least three of the following 15 criteria in the past 12 months from any of the categories below, with at least one criterion present in the past 6 months:

Aggression to people and animals

1 Often bullies, threatens, or intimidates others.
2 Often initiates physical fights.
3 Has used a weapon that can cause serious physical harm to others (e.g., a bat, brick, broken bottle, knife, gun).
4 Has been physically cruel to people.
5 Has been physically cruel to animals.
6 Has stolen while confronting a victim (e.g., mugging, purse snatching, extortion, armed robbery).
7 Has forced someone into sexual activity.

Destruction of property

8 Has deliberately engaged in fire setting with the intention of causing serious damage.
9 Has deliberately destroyed others' property (other than by fire setting).

Deceitfulness or theft

10 Has broken into someone else's house, building, or car.
11 Often lies to obtain goods or favours or to avoid obligations (i.e., "cons" others).
12 Has stolen items of nontrivial value without confronting a victim (e.g., shoplifting, but without breaking and entering; forgery).

Serious violations of rules

13 Often stays out at night despite parental prohibitions, beginning before age 13 years.
14 Has run away from home overnight at least twice while living in the parental or parental surrogate home, or once without returning for a lengthy period.
15 Is often truant from school, beginning before age 13 years.

(pp. 469–470)

In addition to these symptoms, young people with conduct disorder often exhibit a lack of remorse and of empathy. They are typically unconcerned about their academic and behavioural performance at school, putting in little to no effort and then blaming others for their poor outcomes. Young people with conduct disorders may not express feelings and emotions to others or do so superficially or insincerely. This population typically does not go unnoticed at school, due to the externalising nature of their behaviours.

Children and adolescents spend a majority of their time at school, so school may very well be the first-line responder to the identification and support of mental health issues. This highlights the importance of professional development in this area for teachers and other school staff, to strengthen school-wide responses. Staff need to be culturally aware in their responses, as a person's cultural background will affect how they interpret and respond to life experiences (Multicultural Mental Health Australia, 2004).

Students with chronic illness

Chronic illness can be defined as "a medical condition of extended duration that creates impairment in adaptive behaviour and socially defined roles" (Shaw & McCabe, 2008, p. 74). Students with chronic illness are those with ongoing medical condition(s) or disease or who are medically fragile. Childhood chronic illnesses that may limit a child's educational participation include traumatic brain injury, asthma, cancer, cystic fibrosis, and diabetes (Glang, Ettel, Tyler, & Todis, 2012). In the US, 1.5% of all children are unable to regularly attend school because of chronic illness (Kaffenberger, 2006), and although numbers in the UK and Australia are unavailable, both countries acknowledge the negative effects that chronic illness has on educational achievement (The British Psychological Society, 2016; The Royal Children's Hospital Education Institute, 2015).

Post-high school outcomes for students with chronic illnesses differ by age group and medical condition but are poor across the board. Unfortunately, schools often contribute to these poor outcomes through lack of teacher awareness, under-identification or misidentification of the problem, lack of hospital-school communication, and poor parent-educator relationships (Glang et al., 2012).

Schools are increasingly becoming the primary service providers for this population of students, as funding cuts have caused many hospital stays to be shorter and decreased the number of services for families and rehabilitative care. This puts schools in the position of needing to organise and integrate student learning and support with medical care (Glang et al., 2012). In addition to absenteeism, which adversely affects student achievement, chronic illness may affect a student's ability to learn. How affected a student is by their injury or illness depends upon the age of the student at injury/onset of illness, the severity of injury/illness, and the family environment.

Students with chronic illness often experience difficulties in attention, memory, processing speed, and cognitive deficits. School refusal after health improvement is common, as students feel that catching up is impossible after having fallen far behind their peers academically (Shaw & McCabe, 2008). Chronic illnesses such as cancer, asthma, cystic fibrosis, diabetes, and epilepsy may cause fatigue, lethargy, irritability, and depression, which in turn contribute to lack of motivation. Students with chronic illnesses have social and emotional needs related to their medical conditions, which also negatively impact their academic motivation and performance (Shaw & McCabe, 2008). Behaviour problems are common and are related to the depression, withdrawal, anger control, anxiety, and social rejection commonly associated with chronic illness. The news is not all bad, however, as this group of young people have been found to possess stronger coping skills, show less aggressiveness than their peers, and are more altruistic and resilient.

Students with chronic illnesses may not receive the educational supports and services they need because they are not always identified as students eligible for special education provision (Dettmer, Ettel, Glang, & McAvoy, 2014). Because these students experience high rates of absenteeism due to illness and hospitalisation, it is important that a support plan is developed to remove some of the barriers to success that they encounter. Betz and Redcay (2002) identified some of these barriers as: systemic (related to the service systems themselves); provider (attitudes of doctors and educational providers); familial (low expectations and poor family choice making); or individual (the student himself might not be motivated to engage with education).

Collaboration among parents, health care staff, and schools can reduce the challenges for students when returning to school after extended absences and/or hospitalisation. The effects of chronic illness on school outcomes can be mitigated by linking students and their families to follow-up and ongoing services through well-designed and -implemented hospital-to-school transition plans (Shaw & McCabe, 2008).

Cultural perspectives of disability, mental illness, and chronic illness

How a culture views disability, mental illness, and chronic illness has a major impact on whether and how they access services, including those offered by schools. Literature reveals that although disability, mental illness, and chronic illness are three separate conditions, cultural perceptions of each are consistent across the specific culture being examined (Abdullah & Brown, 2011; Gorman & Cross, 2011; Groce & Zola, 1993; Hidde, Harrington, & Routon-Michelinie Winter, 2013). Although people from Anglo cultures tend to view children with disability, mental illness, or chronic illness more favourably than people from other cultures, each of the three conditions has stigma attached to, regardless of the cultural lens (Abdullah & Brown, 2011). Unite for Sight (2015) discusses the effects of this stigma. Cultural beliefs about disability or illness may cause stigma, which can cause people to be reluctant to marry and reproduce with those who have disability, mental illness, or chronic illness, and this may prevent people from accessing care. African and Native Americans both report negative attitudes toward mental health professionals. In addition to the stigma experienced by people with disabilities or illness in most cultures, many may also experience self-stigma, seeing their disability or mental illness as a personal weakness and being reluctant to seek support from a professional (Mehraby, 2009).

Indigenous people of North America have distrust for the government and its programs, due to a painful history of political pushes to annihilate or assimilate them (Abdullah & Brown, 2011). There are hundreds of tribes, each with its own values and perceptions, but some values are common: being, non-interference, harmony with nature, spirituality, sharing and cooperation, and family. Non-interference means that everything was created and occurs for a purpose, and this purpose should not be interfered with. Everything should be allowed to fulfil its natural intended purpose (Abdullah & Brown, 2011).

People of African descent value group collectivism; the way one person acts affects the whole group, which may cause conflicting attitudes toward people with disability or illness (Abdullah & Brown, 2011). For example, some groups may distance themselves or discriminate against a person with disability or illness, but others may react with sympathy and support, to strengthen the group as a whole. Role flexibility is important, and people with these conditions may not have the capacity to step up and take on another role when necessary. Some may view disability or illness as a lesson from God to teach patience or faith, or they could be viewed as a punishment from God for sins or moral weakness. Many have negative attitudes towards treatment due to stigma.

Asian cultures typically have no separation of mind/body; when something is wrong in the mind, it may manifest as somatic illness (Abdullah & Brown, 2011). These people are more likely to seek help for emotional or physical distress from a traditional healer than a physician. They may believe a mental illness is a punishment from God and is the result of bad deeds in a previous life or indicative of bad genes. Others would attribute the ailments to evil spirits, the result of not respecting ancestors. People with disability and illness in these cultures are devalued, and if one family member has a mental illness, it disgraces the whole family.

Latinos value collectivism, interdependence, and cooperation. These values are in opposition to the values of individualism and autonomy that are typically reflected in intervention and therapy (Abdullah & Brown, 2011). Disability and illness are viewed as weaknesses, and the person experiencing them may be viewed as useless. Family and kindness, dignity and respect are values of this group and emphasise the worth of all; this can be problematic for some people with a disability or mental illness, who may act in way that damage their interpersonal relationships. These conditions are sometimes considered to be an imbalance in equilibrium and leave the onus of cure on the individual. This holds the person with disabilities or illness accountable for their problems. Research shows that stigma was a common reason for Latinos not taking their medications (Abdullah & Brown, 2011).

Middle Eastern people value concealing emotions, family honour, patriarchy, respect for authority, and hospitality. Concealing emotions contributes to the stigma towards those who seek mental health services (Abdullah & Brown, 2011). Admitting to a mental illness or seeking services may bring shame upon the family. The self-disclosure required by therapy may violate both concealing emotions and honouring the family. Mental illness may be due to possession by evil spirits.

Lastly, Caucasians are often excluded from studies on cultural perceptions, but it is important to examine them, as most educational and medical services in the Anglosphere are based on Caucasian values, which include individualism, materialism, competition, and future time orientation (Abdullah & Brown, 2011). Independence and autonomy are important. Although generally more accepting than other cultures, these values could cause stigma towards those who require support from others to be successful. Western societies often see disability and mental illness as running in the blood or gene pool, hence the eugenics movement of the past (Groce & Zola, 1993).

Hidde et al. (2013) describe two constructs of disability – reification, where the disability is a feature in the person, and social constructionist, where a condition only becomes a disability when it affects an area that places the individual at a significant disadvantage in a particular environment. Professionals and lay people alike in the US tend to view disability through the reification lens, while those who belong to other societies, such as Australia and the UK, hold views that are predominantly social constructionist. Again, these views will differ based on culture.

Groce and Zola (1993) surmised that three factors are universal in the research on cultural perceptions of disability or illness:

1 Perception of cause of an illness or disability determines a family's or culture's attitudes towards it.
2 Expectations for survival of the child affect how he or she is cared for and how much effort is given to future planning.
3 Expected social roles for children with a disability and/or chronic illness determine the amount of effort and resources a family and community invest in that child, including the areas of education, social participation, autonomy, and lifespan transition planning.

Although their research was conducted over 25 years ago, these universal factors are still evident in the current research literature. Mehraby (2009) stated that although different cultures view mental illness differently, it is usually viewed through religious and spiritual lenses. This may cause people to attribute cause to: (a) possession by demons or spirits, (b) a curse or witchcraft, (c) a holy message from God, (d) punishment for sinning, or (e) punishment for misdeeds in a previous life. These perceived causes may make the family feel ashamed and may leave them socially isolated. This, in turn, may make them reluctant to access services for fear it will call attention to the disability or illness. Parents may hide the affected child away so the chances of siblings being able to marry are not ruined.

Low expectations of survival for children with severe disabilities or illness impacts the availability of support resources and parental attention. Neglecting or overprotecting have negative impacts on psychological development and future planning, which is an issue, as children with disabilities and chronic illness are living longer, most well into their adulthood.

Societal expectations for social roles of children with disability or illness dictates vocational roles and social participation. If the expectation is that the child will not have much, if anything, to contribute to society as an adult, then education and treatment may be neglected. Gender may dictate how much effort is put in for a child's medical care or education, depending on cultural views on gender. These expectations and actions can have negative economic and social implications. Cultural values that contribute to stigma must be examined in order to help mediate that stigma.

Implications for practice

In order to effectively support students with disabilities, mental illness, and chronic illness, educators need to incorporate knowledge about culturally based disability and health beliefs and practices. Education must be accessible and appropriate to all and should address specific culture-related needs (Gorman & Cross, 2011). Education in the Anglosphere, like health care, is based on scientific knowledge but will not be effective unless students and families believe in interventions and the education professionals designing and implementing plans, so ethnocentrism must be avoided. Effective communication is key, and cultural differences can pose a barrier here. To overcome these barriers, the following are suggested:

- Use an approach to assessment that acknowledges diverse cultures (culture-specific instruments are preferred).
- Get to know the person's world view and cultural belief systems about disability, mental health, and illness.
- Give careful explanations for the purpose of any assessments and interventions
- Credibility can be achieved in a number of ways, from making your qualifications clear to taking the time to listen to people's stories and respecting differences.
- Teachers and other school staff should obtain cultural knowledge continuously.
- Listen to family and what their vision for their child is.
- Recognise that the extended family is important in many cultures; include these relatives and allow them to make decisions on the child's behalf, if that is the family's wish.
- Keep in mind that self-determination of children is discouraged in some cultures.

Educators must make decisions on how important it is to introduce an intervention that is not aligned with a student's family culture. The social validity of the intervention must be considered – is it always important to insist on science? If a child's basic human rights are being violated, then advocate for a change. Determine if the child is being treated differently due to disability, mental illness, or chronic illness by comparing the treatment to that of a typically developing child in that culture. Remember that traditional beliefs may change when new information is introduced, but the information must be presented in a culturally responsive manner. Provide parents with the most recent and accurate information possible to assist them in making informed decisions.

It would be remiss to speak about disabilities, mental health, and chronic health problems in relation to schools in the current climate without recognising that immigrants and refugees may have specific issues that must be acknowledged and addressed (Commonwealth of Australia, 2005). Parents and students from this group may experience stress due to culture shock. Organising housing, health care, employment, and education for their families may be stressful for parents, especially if they are without family and friend networks. Language barriers can compound these issues. Refugees may have experienced trauma from war, natural disasters, or torture. These experiences put them at higher risk of developing mental illness such as PTSD, anxiety, and depression.

Supporting students in a multi-tiered culturally responsive system of support

Tier 1 (universal) supports

This equates to examining content, pedagogy, extracurricular activities, and interactions of staff and students. It is also crucial to look at the school's procedures for grouping and labelling students and how achievement gaps and referrals for special education services are conducted. Universal screenings of student progress academically and behaviourally are conducted three times a year to identify students who need additional support (NASP, 2009). These screenings ensure that all students have access to the general education curriculum regardless of educational and behavioural needs, race, culture, or socioeconomic status. The assessments should include culturally responsive behavioural checklists and curriculum-based measurements.

It is important that a validated curriculum is chosen and used in each content area. These curricula must have evidence that academic performance will improve when they are implemented with fidelity (Lane, Menzies, Ennis, & Bezdek, 2013). The teacher's role here is to do this, while at the same time employing *equity pedagogy* and *content integration* to differentiate their instruction to meet the academic, behavioural, and cultural needs of a diverse student population. This is done through the provision of multiple means of representation, action and expression, and engagement. These means should always include examples that represent a variety of cultures, so that all students feel included. *Knowledge construction* is an important part of culturally responsive curriculum implementation. Students learn how content area subject matter is constructed from diverse racial and social class perspectives rather than solely from the dominant Euro-American models.

Tier 1 may include social supports such as evidence-based character development programs to teach social skills or prevent violence. These should fit the particular needs of the school such as decreasing bullying or increasing social skills

(Lane et al., 2013). Although the *reduction of prejudice* should be a result of cultural responsiveness being infused into the Tier 1 screening and implementation activities, character development programs can also be used to give students a voice in the discussion and examination of cultural and racial bias.

Behaviourally, Tier 1 of the MTCRSS is strongly aligned with the PBIS framework and includes the provision of three to five universal expectations for student conduct. These are determined by collecting data from all building staff about what behaviours they think students need to have to be successful in all parts of the school. The expectations are explicitly taught, incorporating opportunities for students to practice and receive coaching and reinforcement through behaviour-specific praise. Depending on the needs of the students, this may include a school-wide or classroom token economy where a token is given with the praise (Lane et al., 2013). Teachers proactively teach and encourage students to meet the behavioural expectations. Although it may sound as if this would take time from academic instruction, it will, in reality, decrease the amount of instructional time teachers lose while attending to problem behaviours.

Tier 2: secondary prevention for some

Tier 2 is implemented in the general education classroom and designed via collaboration with various stakeholders, including the student and family. Tier 2 supports typically take the form of small group evidence-based interventions. These interventions include *equity pedagogy*, in the form of native language support, as well as valuing language and culture (Bianco & Harris, 2014). The school MTCRSS team identifies what resources are already available at the school that can be used for Tier 2 supports and then adds more if necessary. Examples of Tier 2 academic interventions include repeated readings to improve oral fluency, increased practice opportunities in literacy and numeracy, targeted instruction with explicit instruction and modelling, increased teaching for generalisation, guided instruction, more daily review activities, and study skills groups. Teachers should insure that *multicultural content* is integrated in these activities. Social interventions include social skills groups and conflict resolution groups. Behavioural supports are more individually focused and include contracts, self-monitoring, and check in/check out systems, modelling, guided practice, coaching, corrective feedback, peer-mediation, and self-monitoring (Lane et al., 2013). These supports are the ideal place to include *knowledge construction*, *prejudice reduction*, and *empowerment* activities. Overall, the supports in this tier include more exposure, more time, and more opportunities to learn.

Tier 2 is not meant to replace the evidence-based core curricula delivered in Tier 1; rather, it should supplement and enhance student learning. Team members consider students' language, experiences, preferred ways of interacting, and home practices and integrate these factors into intervention development, and both formative and summative progress monitoring. Tier 2 intervention is of particular importance in kindergarten and may prevent the need for more intensive intervention in the future. In secondary school, Tier 2 intervention is focused on remediation and content-specific recovery.

The short-term goal of Tier 2 supports is for students to pass their courses, while graduation is the long-term goal. Teachers provide students with more frequent reinforcement for meeting expectations and instruction in and opportunities to practice academic, behavioural or social skills. This tier typically includes 6–20 weeks of intervention. At the end of the predetermined intervention period, students can receive more Tier 2 intervention, discontinue Tier 2 intervention or add more intensive intervention at Tier 3 (Stobier & Gettinger, 2016). Movement between the tiers is determined through data-based decision making, and it is important to note that when moving up a tier, the supports from the previous tiers are not abandoned, but supplemented. When conducting student assessments, it is of great importance to take into account students' level of acculturation and recognise that cultural differences may impact student achievement and behaviour.

Tier 3: tertiary prevention for a few

Tier 3 interventions are customised for individual students with multiple risk factors who are struggling in multiple areas and are still not meeting outcomes despite receiving Tier 1 and Tier 2 supports. Tier 3 requires more time and resources, because these interventions are implemented by an expert, such as a reading specialist, special education teacher, or counsellor. Progress monitoring is also more frequent to enable better response to student needs. Due to their high academic, social, and/or behavioural support needs, students that need the intensive support of this tier will probably require multiple years of this level of support (Stobier & Gettinger, 2016).

Tier 3 contains the most intensive interventions; most are individual strategies. Behavioural interventions at this level are typically based on functional behaviour assessment. The data from the assessment is used to design a multicomponent support plan targeting several variables. Evidence-based interventions are matched to functions and include token economies, positive and negative consequences, and the extinction of inappropriate behaviours. Again, all involved should be mindful to incorporate *multicultural content*. The student and the family should have a voice in the planning of any behavioural interventions, to ensure consistency between school and home, and *equity pedagogy*. Academic interventions include special education services and evidence-based interventions. Intervention effectiveness should be monitored closely.

Cultural responsiveness at this tier also involves consideration of not only what supports students receive, but who provides them and where they are provided (Klinger & Edwards, 2006). In the best-case scenario, this may mean that supports such as scaffolded instruction are provided in the general education classroom by special and general educators as well as medical and mental health personnel.

Conclusion

Students with disabilities, mental health issues, and chronic illness typically have specific educational, social, and behavioural needs that are different from that of their peers. School leaders, teachers, and support personnel must possess knowledge of these needs and how to best support these students in a culturally responsive way. Supports should begin at a universal level and become more intensive as necessary, determined by data collection, that is, assessment in the areas of students' academic, social, and behavioural domains. Educators can use the Multi-Tiered Culturally Competent System of Support (MTCCSS) to guide their student support efforts to ensure that the practices they implement are not only evidence-based but also culturally relevant and responsive.

References

Abdullah, T., & Brown, T. L. (2011). Mental illness stigma and ethnocultural beliefs, values, and norms: An integrative review. *Clinical Psychology Review, 31*, 934–948.

American Psychiatric Association (APA). (2013). *Diagnostic and statistical manual of mental disorders: DSM-5*. Washington, DC: American Psychiatric Association.

Anxiety and Depression Association of America (ADAA). (2016). *Childhood anxiety disorders*. Retrieved from https://adaa.org/living-with-anxiety/children/childhood-anxiety-disorders

Australian Bureau of Statistics (ABS). (2014). *4427.0 – young people with disability, 2012*. Retrieved from www.abs.gov.au/ausstats/abs@.nsf/Lookup/4427.0main+features152012

Betz, C. L., & Redcay, G. (2002). Lessons learned from providing transition services to adolescents with special health care needs. *Issues in Comprehensive Pediatric Nursing, 25*(2), 129–149.

Bianco, M., & Harris, B. (2014). Strength-based RTI. *Gifted Child Today, 37*(3), 169–176.

The British Psychological Society. (2016). *Behaviour change: School attendance, exclusion and persistent absence*. Retrieved from https://beta.bps.org.uk/sites/beta.bps.org.uk/files/Policy%20-%20Files/Behaviour%20Change%20-%20School%20attendance%2C%20exclusion%20and%20persistent%20absence%20%282017%29.pdf

Commonwealth of Australia. (2005). *Multicultural issues and mental health: Response ability*. Retrieved from www.responseability.org/__data/assets/pdf_file/0009/4797/Multicultural-Issues-and-Mental-Health.pdf

Dettmer, J., Ettel, D., Glang, A., & McAvoy, K. (2014). Building statewide infrastructure for effective educational services for students with TBI: Promising practices and recommendations. *Journal of Head Trauma Rehabilitation, 29*(3), 224–232.

Fuglei, M. (2014). Culturally responsive teaching: Empowering students through respect. *Room241*. Portland, OR: Concordia University. Retrieved from: https://education.cu-portland.edu/blog/classroom-resources/culturally-responsive-teaching-empowering-students-through-respect/

Glang, A., Ettel, D., Tyler, J., & Todis, B. (2012). Educational issues and school reentry for students with traumatic brain injury [Ch. 37]. In N. Zasler, D., Katz, R. Zafonte, D. B. Arciniegas, M. R. Bullock, & J. S. Kreutzer (Eds.), *Brain injury medicine, 2nd edition: Principles and practice*. New York, NY: Demos Medical Publishing.

Gorman, D., & Cross, W. (2011). Cultural issues in mental health. In K-L. Edwards, I. Munro, A. Robins, & A. Welch (Eds.), *Mental health nursing: Dimensions of praxis*. Oxford: Oxford University Press.

GOV.UK. (2014). *Disability prevalence estimates 2002/03 to 2011/12 (Apr to Mar).* Retrieved from www.gov.uk/government/statistics/disability-prevalence-estimates-200203-to-201112-apr-to-mar

GOV.UK. (2017). *Children with Special Educational Needs and Disabilities (SEND).* Retrieved from www.gov.uk/children-with-special-educational-needs

Groce, N. E., & Zola, I. K. (1993). Multiculturism, chronic illness, and disability. *Pediatrics, 95*(5), 1048–1055.

Henley, M., Ramsey, R. S., & Algozzine, R. F. (2008). *Characteristics and strategies for teaching students with mild disabilities.* Upper Saddle River, NJ: Pearson Higher Education.

Hidde, L. A., Harrington, K., & Routon-Michelinie Winter, K. (2013). *Cultural perspectives on disability.* Portland State University Multicultural Topics in Communications Sciences and Disorders. Retrieved from www.pdx.edu/multicultural-topics-communication-sciences-disorders/

Kaffenberger, C. (2006). School reentry for students with chronic illness: A role for professional counselors. *Professional School Counselling, 9,* 223–230.

Klinger, J. K., & Edwards, P. A. (2006). Cultural considerations with response to intervention models. *Reading Research Quarterly, 41*(1), 108–117.

Lane, K. L., Menzies, H. M., Ennis, R. P., & Bezdek, J. (2013). School-wide systems to promote positive behaviours and facilitate instruction. *Journal of Curriculum and Instruction,* 7(1), 6–31.

Lawrence, D., Johnson, S., Hafekost, J., Boterhoven de Haan, K., Sawyer, M., Ainley, J., & Zubrick, S. R. (2015). *The mental health of children and adolescents.* Report on the second Australian Child and Adolescent Survey of Mental Health and Wellbeing. Canberra: Australian Government Department of Health. Retrieved from www.health.gov.au/internet/main/publishing.nsf/Content/9DA8CA21306FE6EDCA257E2700016945/%24File/child2.pdf

March, J., Silva, S., Petrycki, S., Curry, J., Wells, K., Fairbank, J., . . . Severe, J. (2004). Fluoxetine, cognitive-behavioral therapy, and their combination for adolescents with depression: Treatment for Adolescents with Depression Study (TADS) randomized controlled trial. *Journal of the American Medical Association, 292*(7), 807–820.

Mehraby, N. (2009). Possessed or crazy? Mental illness across cultures. *Psychotherapy in Australia, 15*(2), 43.

Multicultural Mental Health Australia. (2004). *Reality check: Culturally diverse mental health consumers speak out.* Retrieved from www.mmha.org.au/MMHAPublications/Store/realitycheck/view

National Association of School Psychologists (NASP). (2009). *Appropriate academic supports to meet the needs of all students.* Position Statement. Author, Bethesda, MD.

National Center for Education Statistics (NCES). (2017). *Children and youth with disabilities.* Retrieved from https://nces.ed.gov/programs/coe/indicator_cgg.asp

Psychology Today. (2017). *Depressive disorders (children and adolescents).* Retrieved from www.psychologytoday.com/conditions/depressive-disorders-children-and-adolescents#symptoms

The Royal Children's Hospital Education Institute. (2015). *An Australian and New Zealand review of education support for children with chronic health conditions.* Retrieved from www.rch.org.au/uploadedFiles/Main/Content/education/National%20Review%20of%20Hospital%20Based%20Education%20Support.pdf

Shaw, S., & McCabe, P. (2008). Hospital-to-school transition for children with chronic illness: Meeting the new challenges of an evolving health care system. *Psychology in the Schools, 45*(1), 74–87.

Stobier, K. C., & Gettinger, M. (2016). Multi-tiered systems of support and evidence-based practices. In S. R. Jimerson, M. K. Burns, & A. M. VanDerHeyden (Eds.), *Handbook of response to intervention* (pp. 121–141). New York, NY: Springer Publishing.

Unite for Sight. (2015). *Module 7: Cultural perspectives on mental health*. Retrieved from www.uniteforsight.org

The United Nations. (2006). Convention on the rights of persons with disabilities. *Treaty Series, 2515*, 3.

5

AT-RISK STUDENTS

Students in out-of-home care, involvement with the juvenile justice system, and from low SES backgrounds

Introduction

Young people that are engaged with the juvenile justice and/or out-of-home (foster) care systems are often from low socioeconomic status (SES) backgrounds and have a disability, and therefore are involved with multiple systems of support. Because of these factors, they have unique support needs that likely require collaboration with professionals from education, disability, social work, and juvenile justice. Students with complex needs such as these may transition in and out of their home schools from juvenile justice, as well as frequently changing schools due to foster home placement changes. This increases the challenge that educators and other professionals face keeping these youths engaged in school and providing them with a quality education. Many of these challenges can be addressed through the provision of culturally responsive practices, such as interagency collaboration, transition planning, and a multi-tiered system of supports. While evidence-based practices have been identified as effective for this population, a significant gap between theory and practice remains. Systemic changes are needed to address this gap.

It must also be noted that young people of colour and indigenous people (those who are descended from and identify with the original inhabitants of a given region) are overrepresented in these three conditions and underrepresented in life areas that are protective factors, such as education, employment, and housing. For example, in Australia, indigenous people identify themselves as having Aboriginal or Torres Strait Islander descent and make up 3.3% of the population (ABS, 2017). This population is underrepresented in education (57.9% of teens attending school), earnings (indigenous people still receive a personal income that is only two-thirds that of the non-indigenous population), and housing (only 39.6% own their own home, and overcrowding is significantly higher than in the white population) (ABS, 2017). Compounding these issues, young Aboriginal people are overrepresented in the juvenile justice and out-of-home care systems. The Young Report describes a similar a pattern of multiple disadvantage in areas of social policy for young black and Muslim men in the UK, particularly around disproportionality in the justice system (Clinks, 2014). In the US, young people of colour are significantly over-represented in both the juvenile justice and foster care systems (U.S. Department of Justice, 2017; U.S. Department of Health and Human Services, 2016). There is also evidence of socioeconomic, racial/ethnic, and gender inequalities in academic achievement (Becares & Priest, 2015).

Globally, socioeconomic status has the largest effect of the factors mentioned earlier, many times predicating involvement with juvenile justice and out-of-home care (United Nations, 2016). Socioeconomic status is calculated not only on income but also educational attainment, occupation, and perceptions of social status/class (American Psychological Association, n.d.). It has been shown to be a predictor of a variety of life outcomes, including physical and psychological health (Richards, Garratt, & Heath, 2016), and thus requires further examination when exploring the characteristics and support needs of the complex needs of at-risk students.

The groups of students highlighted in this chapter have individual hurdles to overcome and unique support needs, as many young people are involved in two or more of the situations discussed. This chapter offers a holistic view of these at-risk youth and makes research-based suggestions of how to support them using the multi-tiered culturally responsive system of support presented in Chapter 2.

Students from low socioeconomic backgrounds

When describing students with low socioeconomic status (SES), one is generally referring to the student and his or her family's income, education, occupational prestige, social status, and social class (APA, 2017). Many associate SES with poverty, but poverty is more finite; therefore, SES is the more comprehensive and reliable predictor of life outcomes, including physical and psychological health (APA, 2017). Measures of SES differ according to who is collecting the data and its purpose. Often, particularly when exploring the outcomes of young people, SES is measured in relation to a geographical area (for example, using postcodes); this can be inappropriate, as individuals and families may differ greatly from their neighbours.

The Australian Bureau of Statistics uses the following to measure SES: (a) consumption; (b) demographics such as marital status, native language, and English proficiency; (c) highest level of educational attainment; (d) employment status (the young person, parents, and other family members); (e) family size and composition; (f) health, including disability, mental health, and alcohol/other drug support needs; (g) income of the young person, parents, and/or household; (h) geographic location (rural, remote, suburbs, city); (i) wealth, including young person and parents' occupations, home ownership, car ownership, and Internet access; and (j) community, referring to either the young person's residential or school community.

The SES of school students is often measured to determine and influence outcomes. SES has been shown to be one of the most accurate predictors of life outcomes; low SES is correlated with low educational achievement, poverty, and poor health (APA, 2017). The American Psychological Association (2017) lists psychological, physical, educational, and family outcomes that are affected by SES. Students with low SES are prone to high levels of emotional disabilities, delinquent behaviour, ADHD, depression, anxiety, attempted suicide, cigarette smoking, and drug and alcohol dependence in adolescence. Physically, low SES has been associated with higher infant mortality, obesity, chronic stressful experiences, and the likelihood that young people will be sedentary. The latter may be attributed to a lack of resources such as playgrounds and gyms (APA, 2017).

Educationally, low SES backgrounds may have negative impacts on students' academic success, learning (linguistic, cognitive, socioemotional skills), behaviour, and health. This population of students often commences kindergarten with lower linguistic knowledge, achieves lower scores on national achievement tests, and experiences high absenteeism and dropout rates (APA, 2017).

Richards et al. (2016) conducted a study to determine if the situation in the UK was as dismal as the situation in the US for young people with low SES. They discovered that the picture in the UK was not as bad as what has been reported in the US; along with areas of concern were areas of improvement and narrowing gaps of inequality. They found that although there were widening inequalities in respect to SES in some of the same areas listed by the APA (misbehaviour, emotional disorders, ADHD), they also found that the gaps were closing in other areas, such as truancy, parental engagement with school and homework, and the frequency with which mothers read to their children.

Schools are often structured in a way that is best suited to middle-class norms and values. Teachers may assume that parents are home in the evenings and not realise that even young students may have serious responsibilities such as watching and caring for younger siblings. This can lead teachers to erroneously thinking that students have a disability or are lazy, unmotivated, or apathetic about school and homework. The IRIS Center (2012) describes some challenges that students from low SES backgrounds may experience, such as: (a) having even their basic needs met, (b) lack of books, computers, and Internet at home, (c) limited access to transportation, (d) reduced access and opportunity to participate in extracurricular and community activities, (e) homelessness or transiency, (f) malnutrition, (g) lack of access to health care, (h) a place to do homework and assistance with it, (i) less supervision and more responsibilities at home, and (j) poor sleeping patterns.

Students may be dealing with one or more of these challenges, and they may contribute to difficulties in school, such as remaining engaged, as they may have difficulty staying awake and concentrating. Because of increased responsibilities, students from low SES backgrounds may find it difficult to get to school on time or get there at all. This may, in turn, affect their ability to stay in school and graduate. Students who experience low levels of parental supervision at home may not communicate well with others and thereby have difficulty appropriately responding to and forming bonds with peers and authority figures. Often these students have an independent mindset, which may cause tension in the classroom, particularly around group activities.

Students involved with the juvenile justice system

Statistics in Australia, New Zealand, the UK, and the US show that most young people (85%) that are involved with the juvenile justice system are actually supervised in the community rather than held in detention (AIHW, 2016; NZ Stats, 2017; Ministry of Justice, 2017; Sedlak & Bruce, 2016). In Australia, most of these (80%) were males between 14 and 17 years old, 40% of these were indigenous, and they spent an average of six months under supervision (AIHW, 2016). Statistics from New Zealand paint a similar picture; 80% were males between the ages of 15–16, and 63% were indigenous (NZ Stats, 2017). The Youth Justice System (YJS) in the UK is structured to address the needs of young people under the age of 18. This appears to be having a positive effect, as there have been significant reductions in first-time offenders (83%), the total number or youth receiving cautions (81%), and custodial sentences (66%) (Ministry of Justice, 2017).

These students have many unique characteristics and experiences that may require supports across the three tiers of a multi-tiered culturally responsive system of support (MTCRSS). They generally experience multiple forms of social disadvantage, such as homelessness, incarcerated family members, family dysfunction, alcohol and drug misuse, and involvement in the out-of-home care system (Cumming, Strnadová, & Dowse, 2014). This population also experiences higher rates of intellectual disability, mental health disorders, speech, language, and communication difficulties, specific learning difficulties, and social, emotional, and behavioural difficulties (Gagnon & Richards, 2008). Young people with disabilities have a higher rate of offending and incarceration and more difficulty reintegrating to the community than their typically developing peers (Dowse, Cumming, Strnadová, Lee, & Trofimovs, 2014). Dowse, Baldry, and Snoyman (2009) found that these individuals are at high risk of becoming caught in a cycle of social exclusion and criminalisation early in their lives, resulting in their involvement in the criminal justice system, incarceration, and recidivism.

Students involved with the justice system often become disengaged from school early (Strnadová, O'Neill, & Cumming, 2017). This results in high rates of truancy, which, in turn, results in low levels of literacy and numeracy. They typically present with serious behavioural challenges, resulting in delinquency, which has been shown to negatively impact academic performance (Brooks & Tarling, 2012). Grigorenko et al. (2015) found that only 4.8% of juvenile detainees perform at or above their grade level in word-level reading, 22.8% for text-level reading, and 13.8% for mathematics computation and reasoning. A similar study conducted by Maddern (2009) found that out of the 150,000 of juvenile detainees in the UK, one-third need help with reading and writing, and 15% have statements of special educational needs, compared with about 3% of the general population. These statistics underscore the need for a system that mitigates these issues by simultaneously addressing students' cultural, academic, and behavioural needs, along with effective transition planning.

The majority of these students experience poor outcomes upon their release and return to community, including a lack of engagement with education and employment and high rates of recidivism (Strnadová et al., 2017). Clark and Unruh (2010) suggest that for many incarcerated young people, returning home is sometimes more difficult than being locked up; education, the community, employers, housing, health care, and other treatment may not be welcoming or available. For many, it is counterproductive to return to the environment of complex disadvantage that fostered the behaviours that put them there in the first place. Clark and Unruh further propose that effective transition planning may be the most critical part of any program to mitigate these factors and foster positive outcomes for incarcerated youth with disabilities.

Students in out-of-home care

Out-of-home care (OOHC) typically refers to the placement of children and young people who are unable to live with their primary caregivers with alternative short- or long-term carers (AIFS, 2017). It is also referred to as foster care. This arrangement is sometimes arranged informally, through other family members or friends, or formally through the courts. Providing support to families so that children and young people can reside safely in their family homes is the preferred option, with OOHC being a last resort. There are several different types and categories of OOHC, ranging from emergency short-term to long-term care (see Table 5.1 for details). The OOHC systems in the Anglosphere face many

TABLE 5.1 Types of out-of-home care placements

Emergency	A safe placement for a few nights.
Short respite	Regular stays with a family by children and young people who have a disability or behavioural difficulties to give their parents/carers short breaks.
Residential care	Placement in a building where there are staff paid to provide a stable residential environment for children and young people. Previously known as orphanages.
Family group homes	Homes for children designated and supported by a government department or community agency who have live-in carers who are subsidised for the provision of care.
Home-based care	Children are placed in the home of carers who are reimbursed for the cost of caring for the child. This category includes foster care, relative care, and third-party parental care.
Independent living	Young people are placed into private board or lead tenant households.
Other	Other placements such as hospitals, hotels, and boarding schools.

Source: Australian Institute of Health and Welfare (AIHW, 2017, p. 47); GOV.UK (n.d.), National Center for Mental Health Promotion and Youth Violence Prevention (2010)

challenges, including limited numbers of foster parents to provide quality care for children and young people, inadequate resources, and problems providing support to relatives who act as carers (National Center for Mental Health Promotion and Youth Violence Prevention, 2010; Senate Community Affairs Committee, 2015).

There are several reasons why a young person would be placed in OOHC. These include parental abuse and/or neglect, parental incarceration, or voluntary relinquishment of parental rights (National Center for Mental Health Promotion and Youth Violence Prevention, 2010). A judge or other government body typically makes a recommendation that the child either be removed from the home or remain in the home with support services. If the decision is to remove the child from the home, there is typically a protective or custody hearing with a judge. If the judge determines that there has been abuse or neglect, custody is normally granted to and follows the recommendation of the child welfare agency regarding placement. The family is then assigned a caseworker, who develops a case plan that focuses on short-term care and the steps that parents must take to reach the goal of family reunification (National Center for Mental Health Promotion and Youth Violence Prevention, 2010).

Palmieri and LaSalle (2016) disclose some worrying statistics about students in OOHC. They typically experience social-emotional, behavioural, and academic challenges at school. They are twice as likely to have high rates of absenteeism and be the recipients of exclusionary discipline practices, such as out of school suspension. They are three and a half times more likely to require special education supports. A quarter of all foster children have been suspended or expelled at least once. The behavioural difficulties these students display can be attributed to a number of things, but one significant contributor is their high level of school mobility. Most have changed schools upon entering care, and over a third experience five or more school changes over their educational careers. Multiple school placements result in gaps in student learning and negatively affect their academic success, and students with special needs sometimes lose services when they change schools (Heffernan, 2010).

Early attachment disruptions are also a contributor to both behavioural difficulties and in forming and sustaining relationships with peers and staff. Some students may present with internalising disorders such as fear, anxiety, guilt, and social withdrawal. Learning is a social activity, so these social-emotional challenges have a negative effect on academic achievement (Zetlin, MacLeod, & Kimm, 2012). Teachers may struggle to find ways to support this population of students in their classrooms. Zetlin et al. (2012) discussed challenges that students in OOHC face in contrast to their peers: learning and emotional challenges, weak academic backgrounds, difficulty settling into classroom routines, hyperactivity, anger issues, and problems getting along with peers. Foster parents were not always available to assist the teachers with behavioural or academic issues. Students also missed school for court dates and parental visits. Caregivers contributed to student challenges. Some students had no supplies, money for lunch, poor hygiene, and inadequate clothing. Caregivers often failed to attend parent teacher conferences and meetings, sign paperwork that was sent home, and provide support when contacted by the teacher.

These challenges can translate to negative outcomes. Students in OOHC score 16–20 percentile points below their peers on standardised tests, less than 50 percent finish high school, and only 3% attend post-secondary education after graduation (National Working Group on Foster Care and Education, 2014). Those who grow up in care tend to have challenging behaviours and difficulty maintaining relationships, due to childhood experiences of abuse and trauma and/or mental health issues. Young people who have experienced multiple placements while in care generally experience poorer life outcomes (Beauchamp, 2014). Young people leaving OOHC typically leave school early, and are overrepresented in the statistics on homelessness, involvement with the criminal justice system, teen pregnancy, and having their own children taken into care. They also tend to be unemployed or underemployed, have physical and mental health issues, and misuse alcohol and other substances (Beauchamp, 2014).

Children in OOHC are involved with a variety of people, agencies, and systems, such as: (a) their biological family, (b) foster family or group home, (c) case managers or social workers, (d) school personnel, (e) advocates, (f) court systems, including judges and attorneys, and (g) other agencies, such as mental health, drug and alcohol rehabilitation, therapists, and early childhood workers. The involvement of such a large number of people and agencies can cause barriers and challenges for young people in care; it is therefore paramount that there is collaboration between these entities so that student success is not hampered (Heffernan, 2010).

International studies show that there is an overrepresentation of young people from OOHC in the youth justice system, and many young people leaving OOHC do so via the youth justice system, which leads to even poorer outcomes in social and economic engagement in mainstream society (Mendes, Baidawi, & Snow, 2014). Young people leaving OOHC are one of the most vulnerable and disadvantaged groups; their precare and aftercare experiences leave them susceptible to a number of poor outcomes. Mendes et al. (2014) found individual, environmental, and systemic reasons for the overrepresentation of young people in OOHC in the juvenile justice system, including unresolved trauma and substance abuse, association with offending peers and family involvement in the criminal justice system, school exclusion, instability of the OOHC system, and lack of aftercare support.

Implications for practice

Positive educational experiences can go a long way in countering the abuse, neglect, instability, and other barriers that students in OOHC have experienced (U.S. Department of Education, 2016). Participating in and finishing high school, along with the pursuit of tertiary education, are seen as protective factors for this population, as they enhance their well-being, increase the chance of positive transitions to adulthood, and increase their chances of economic independence (U.S. Department of Education, 2016). The New South Wales Department of Education (n.d.) has provided advice to school leadership teams on improving school experiences for students in OOHC. Principals must make sure that students in OOHC can access and participate in education on the same basis as all students. Students should have their OOHC status recorded on their enrolment and have an educational plan, and it must be reviewed/updated yearly.

Schools should consider employing a multi-tiered culturally responsive system of support (MTCRSS) to address the complex cultural, academic, and behavioural needs of students who are a part of one or more of these populations. This would allow education professionals to use universal screening to assess and identify students that require more support than what is included in the universal tier (Tier 1). Next is a discussion of how a MTCRSS can increase the chances of positive adult outcomes for these vulnerable populations. Although not comprehensive in regards to interventions in each tier, in order to avoid repetition from previous chapters, the next section will describe interventions that are specific to the populations described in this chapter. These include school connectedness; interagency collaboration; social, life, and anger management skills instruction; mental health services; and transition planning.

Supporting students in a multi-tiered culturally responsive system of support

Students from the populations discussed may require additional supports that are unique to their situations. Educators must take more than ethnicity into account when considering cultural responsiveness for these students; these populations of students have their own ideas, customs, and social behaviours developed through their lived experiences.

Tier 1 (universal) supports

Tier 1 supports for the complex needs of this population should be focused around ways to foster school connectedness through an *empowering school culture* and interagency collaboration. The building blocks of positive behaviour support should be included, as they have increased significance to these populations of students: explicitly stated expectations, natural consequences, structured and predictable environments, and individual attention (Palmieri & La Salle, 2016).

McKellar and Cowan (2011) stress the importance of universal assessment at this tier; students should be assessed upon enrolment to determine whether there is a match between the curriculum and the student's ability. Depending on the student's needs, supports can be given that span the three tiers, including high-quality data-informed instruction, tutoring and remedial instruction, social skills, and life skills instruction. Students who are missing credits due to incompatible programs in the juvenile justice system or from missing school due to the instability of residential placements should be provided with the means to make up missing credits.

Palmieri and LaSalle (2016) found that positive support and encouragement for academic success from teachers, other school staff, and caseworkers improved both academic and behavioural outcomes for students in OOHC. This includes taking the time to listen, making the student feel valued, and providing acceptance, encouragement, and motivation. These are the building blocks for the development of positive relationships between students and school staff, which is a major component of school connectedness. School connectedness is an important construct that promotes protective factors and minimises risk factors in order to improve the quality of life and outcomes of young people (CDC, 2009). School connectedness has been known to decrease the chances that students will engage in behaviours that may compromise their well-being and health, as well as increasing their chances of academic success (Cumming, Marsh, & Higgins, 2018). There are many things that schools can do to promote connectedness; the school and its classrooms should be structured and supportive, with daily routines, increased opportunities for practice, and fostering of trusting relationships (McKellar & Cowan, 2011). Encourage the involvement of caregivers and monitor and communicate student progress. Cumming et al. recommend including parents and students in school-wide and educational planning and support them in developing the self-advocacy and self-determination skills that will allow them to do this effectively. To promote connectedness, schools need to assist students in feeling that they are a part of the school community; this can be cultivated by assigning students adult and peer mentors (Zetlin et al., 2012) and encouraging participation in extracurricular activities (Palmieri & LaSalle, 2016).

School leaders should provide school staff with professional learning opportunities in the area of support needs for students involved with the juvenile justice system and/or in OOHC, in a *knowledge construction* approach. This can provide them with a better understanding of why students enter foster care and what their unique needs are, *prejudice reduction*, and increased sensitivity. Zetlin et al. (2012) found that teachers desired professional development to learn how to best support these students in their classrooms. They especially wanted guidance on how to deal with their emotional and behavioural needs and help them to feel comfortable in class. They wanted veteran teacher mentors, as well as more communication and opportunities to collaborate with foster parents and social workers. They expressed the need for knowledge and strategies in the areas of drug and alcohol misuse and runaways. Teachers wanted more information on how the child welfare system works and the laws governing it. They wanted to know how to handle situations such as the child's birth parents showing up at school and what information could be shared and with who. This study highlights the importance of asking staff where their professional development needs lie and supporting them in providing *equity pedagogy* to all of their students.

Schools don't always have the child welfare records of the students, so they don't know the reason that each student was placed in OOHC or a juvenile justice centre. They may also not have the students' previous educational or health records (Palmieri & La Salle, 2016). Despite these barriers, care should be taken to expedite school enrolment processes to reduce the time that students are not attending classes. Every effort should be made to keep the student in the school that s/he was in at the time of residential placement. If the child must be transferred to a different school, enrolment should occur immediately, with all records being provided to the new school.

Collaboration between the education and child welfare sectors is essential to improve the educational outcomes of youth in OOHC (Heffernan, 2010; U.S. Department of Education, 2016). School leaders should aim to enhance collaboration with the child welfare and other systems, as this will go a long way in meeting the educational, mental health, and physical needs of young people in OOHC, and for those transitioning back to school from a juvenile justice setting. This will also allow for the identification of barriers to the educational success of these students and assist in addressing them. Effective collaboration may result in improved sharing of information, fewer school transitions, more timely school enrolment, and limit the number of times that the child has to tell and retell his or her story to strangers, thus enhancing the child's experience of continuity and security (National Center for Mental Health Promotion and Youth Violence Prevention, 2010).

Schools can use a number of strategies to develop this collaboration, the first and foremost being the development of good relationships with senior staff in the child welfare and juvenile justice sectors, as frontline workers typically have high turnover rates. Senior staff members can guide their staff to collaborate with school staff on issues concerning students in OOHC, as well as enabling policy changes and decision making. Another important strategy is the development of guidelines to facilitate information sharing across systems. Memorandums of understanding can be developed that outline what information is shared, how it is shared, and with whom it is shared (O'Neill, Strnadová, & Cumming, 2017). A universal consent and confidentiality form can smooth and expedite the flow of information between systems. Each agency's role should be clearly defined, and all involved should have knowledge of each other's roles. This can be further strengthened by cross-training professional development offered by each system to share policies, procedures, skills, and perspectives (National Center for Mental Health Promotion and Youth Violence Prevention, 2010). This may assist in reducing tensions and building partnerships between organisations and improve service delivery for students in OOHC and their families. Regular case management meetings that involve representatives from each system will ensure that students receive all of their needed supports.

Classroom practices

Gorski (2008) claims that the most important first step that teachers can take to improve their support of students from low SES backgrounds is to examine their own perceptions and how these shape their practice. Despite research to the contrary, several damaging myths persist about poverty and class. These include: people with low SES are unmotivated and lack a strong work ethic and do not value education and therefore are uninvolved in their children's learning, are linguistically deficient, and tend to misuse drugs and alcohol (Gorski, 2008). These are, of course, untrue, as the majority of students from low SES backgrounds have at least one working parent; low SES parents hold the same attitudes about education that wealthy parents do; all people, no matter their language, speak structured language with complex grammatical structures; and poor people are actually less likely than their wealthy counterparts to abuse alcohol or drugs (Gorski, 2008). Gorski further highlights that educators need to stop perpetuating classism and the myths associated with it by doing away with practices such as ability grouping and deficit thinking and educating themselves about class and poverty. Teachers should involve families as much as possible and not be judgemental if parents/carers appear to be unresponsive.

Students with low SES are individuals and therefore do not face the same challenges or respond to them in the same manner. Teachers need to get to know their students and build relationships with them so they can identify and appropriately respond to students' needs (The IRIS Center, 2012). Although this is good advice for all teachers, it is especially helpful for students with complex needs, as they are likely to be disengaged from school and can benefit from strong relationships with teachers and having their strengths and interests capitalised upon through *equity pedagogy* and *multicultural content integration*, so that learning is more relevant to them. It is helpful to provide students with a wealth of resources and support (e.g., identifying people with different areas of expertise at the school who can support students in meeting their basic needs by linking them and their families to supports and services).

Teachers should also ensure that they are implementing evidence-based Tier 1 practices for all students, as these are particularly crucial to the populations of students described in this chapter. The basic building block to Tier 1 interventions is to create a structured and well-managed classroom. Consistent classroom routines and schedules will help students to feel less anxious, which is very important for students who already have uncertain and stressful lives. These are supports that facilitate an *empowering* classroom culture. Self-regulation strategies, such as self-monitoring, can support students in regulating their own behaviour, increasing their self-actualisation and self-determination skills (Regan & Michaud, 2011). Students could also benefit from social skills instruction, to assist them in appropriate social communication, raise their self-esteem, and teach them how to handle their emotions (Regan & Michaud, 2011). *Prejudice reduction* and *knowledge construction* activities are valuable components of this instruction.

Teachers should activate prior knowledge and integrate *multicultural content* to make instruction relevant to students' lives. Vocabulary instruction and the use of graphic organisers can support students in acquiring language and communication skills. Provide students with increased opportunities to respond and give them timely and frequent feedback. Provide instruction in smaller chunks to assist with retention and avoid student frustration (The IRIS Center, 2012).

Students experiencing the challenges discussed in this chapter likely do not receive an abundance of positive reinforcement outside of school. Extrinsic reward systems such as token economies, along with frequent, specific praise, can assist students to build confidence and intrinsic motivation as they learn academic and social skills (Regan & Michaud, 2011). Tailoring instruction to include students' interests and practical applications will help to engage students and support them in understanding how the content is related to their lives (The IRIS Center, 2012).

Zetlin et al. (2012) suggests that once teachers know their students, they can make some universal accommodations as part of *equity pedagogy* that acknowledge and account for the cultural differences and experiences of students with complex needs. One example is to adjust writing assignments to allow students to write about themselves rather than their families and replace holiday reminiscing with less painful topics. Terminology changes, for example, using the word "adults" rather than "parents", and including non-traditional households when discussing families. These are examples of how *multicultural content integration* can support these populations. Students from low SES backgrounds, involved in OOHC and/ or juvenile justice systems often have difficulty finding and accessing resources, such as technology, books, and study spaces. Teachers who use *equity pedagogy* will recognise this and be mindful not to assign outside work that requires this access without providing students with the means to complete it. They can assist students by being available before and after school. Homework clubs that provide access to technology are another good way to provide the means for students to study and complete assignments (The IRIS Center, 2012).

Tier 2: secondary prevention for some

Relational trauma may cause a student with complex needs to have an inability to effectively regulate his or her emotions and behaviours. Emotional and behavioural regulation is required for social and academic success at school. Success in school requires students to be able to pay attention, follow directions, appropriately socialise, and control their emotions, as these skills affect the way students learn. Some students will require support in these areas in order to be successful (Palmieri & LaSalle, 2016). Palmieri and LaSalle (2016) recommend social skills instruction, anger management training, and mindfulness meditation to support the development of these skills. These supports are well aligned with all five of the culturally responsive components of the MTCRSS model.

Social skills instruction is an evidence-based intervention that involves the direct instruction of social skills, delivered via modelling, coaching, and practising (Lane, Menzies, Ennis, & Bezdek, 2013). Students' skills are first assessed, then the intervention is implemented to fill any identified gaps. There are a number of commercially available research-based social skills curricula in existence. Anger management training uses the instruction of related social skills to teach students how to effectively deal with their emotions that lead to angry responses such as verbal and physical aggression. These skills will assist students in developing feelings of *empowerment*, gaining a deeper understanding through *knowledge construction*, and *reducing prejudices*.

Mindfulness meditation is a practice that aims to exercise the mind and make it focused. It is easy to practice, as it does not require any equipment. Its practice can be used to support students in developing an awareness of their mind and body, including any negative thoughts, in a non-reactive and non-judgemental way (Chapman & Mitchell, 2013). Research indicates that mindfulness is associated with greater emotional intelligence and a reduction in depression and aggression (Chapman & Mitchell, 2013). There are a number of ways to implement small group mindfulness instruction, but basically students are introduced to the concept of mindfulness and taught to focus on a particular thing about their bodies, such as their breathing, emotions, or heartbeats.

Students from low SES backgrounds, in OOHC, and involved with the juvenile justice system often have low literacy and numeracy skills (APA, 2017; Strnadová et al., 2017) and may require Tier 2 supports to improve their abilities in these areas. Milson-Black (2017) recommended that all targeted literacy and numeracy intervention follow the same format: a pretest, followed by 8–12 weeks of evidence-based intensive instruction, followed by a post-test. An integral part of these interventions involves supporting the development of students' metacognition by teaching them to talk about their learning and their needs and to self-identify any gaps. Instruction is always guided by assessment and the students' response to the interventions (see Chapter 4 for more specific information about Tier 2 literacy and numeracy interventions). As stated in previous chapters, it is important to remember that Tier 2 supports are typically provided in the general education classroom and are meant to supplement, not replace, the existing Tier 1 supports. Teachers using the MTCRSS are mindful that they are implementing *equity pedagogy* and *integrating multicultural content* when planning these supports.

Tier 3: tertiary prevention for a few

Palmieri and La Salle (2016) recommend that schools recognise the unique needs of these students; their social-emotional and cultural needs must be taken into account, as they form the basis of students' well-being and have a direct influence over behavioural and academic success. A school psychologist should assess the student to determine his or her unique needs, then, in collaboration with the student, design culturally responsive supports to meet those needs. The school psychologist should focus on the student's strengths, rather than deficits. Some students in OOHC show great resiliency, and positive school experiences have been shown to contribute to resilience and feelings of *empowerment* and can help students to recover from trauma (Palmieri & La Salle, 2016). Some students may benefit from counselling and other mental health services – trauma focused cognitive behavioural therapy and therapy for depression (McKellar & Cowan, 2011).

Individualised transition planning is another area that is strongly recommended for students involved with juvenile justice and OOHC systems. These students often experience more transitions than their peers, as they may be moving from school to juvenile justice settings, then back to school or from one residential placement and school to others. Effective transition planning and practices are integral to the academic and behavioural success of students involved in one or more of these systems. Schools, in conjunction with child welfare and juvenile justice agencies, can adopt policies to support successful school transitions. These should include those regarding school transportation and its costs, immediate enrolment (even if health and school records have not been produced yet), confidentiality and information sharing, expedited special education meetings, and guidelines outlining the roles and responsibilities of school, OOHC, juvenile justice, and caregivers when enrolling students in a new school (National Center for Mental Health Promotion and Youth Violence Prevention, 2010).

Mendes et al. claim that in order to improve outcomes for young people transitioning out of care, the quality of care and placement stability must be improved, transition planning must be gradual and flexible, and young people must be given continued access to support after care. This aftercare is best structured as wraparound services- coordinated multi-systemic care. This underscores the importance of interagency collaboration as part of the universal tier of support.

Mendes et al. (2014) also found that leaving care plans did not typically address offending behaviours, as this was felt to be the role of the juvenile justice system. Plans were not always implemented, as parole plans were developed as part of the youths' transition out of juvenile justice and back to the community. This highlights the need for plans to be developed collaboratively. Someone from either the juvenile justice school should also be involved in this planning (O'Neill et al., 2017).

Transition planning should include the development of an individual plan that the student has been involved in creating. The student should receive support and training in learning how to do this. Foster and kinship carers should receive training in how to support students as they transition from care. The plan should be reviewed regularly to assess progress being made toward the goals. Planning should address predicted needs as well as immediate ones. The plan should be evidence-based, covering areas detailed in the literature, such as the *Taxonomy for Transition Programming 2.0* (Kohler, Gothberg, Fowler, & Coyle, 2016). The *Taxonomy* provides stakeholders across education, support services, and program practitioners with a research-based model to plan, organise, and evaluate transitions of students with complex needs. The importance of a multi-systemic approach to transition planning and support is apparent by its five primary practice categories: (a) youth-focused planning, (b) youth development, (c) family engagement, (d) program structures, and, (e) interagency collaboration. Within these categories, housing is of particular importance when planning and monitoring after the transition, particularly for young people who have experienced disrupted placements, so that they are not left homeless (McKellar & Cowan, 2011).

Regular meetings should be held with all who are involved with each student, including: teachers, foster parents, staff from other involved agencies (social worker, probation officer, mental health professional, school counsellor, mentor, special educator) to monitor progress on reaching the goals set out in the plan and aftercare services (National Center for Mental Health Promotion and Youth Violence Prevention, 2010).

Conclusion

Students from low SES backgrounds often have complex needs and may also be involved with the juvenile justice and/or out-of-home care systems. Schools can make a significant difference in this population's outcomes by providing them with stability and a place that they feel connected to. When students have developed positive relationships with their peers and school personnel and feel that others care about their social and academic success, it increases their engagement in school, thereby improving their academic outcomes.

Educators should support the complex needs of this population via a multi-tiered culturally responsive system of support. The MTCRSS provides a framework based on data-based decision making to support students' academic and social/behavioural success, all the while taking their unique culture and experiences into account. For this population, supports should be focused on interagency collaboration, school connectedness, social skill instruction, mindfulness, mental health supports, and transition practices.

References

AIHW. (2016). *Young people in child protection and under youth justice supervision 2013–14.* Canberra: AIHW. Data linkage series no. 21. Cat. no. CSI 22.

American Psychological Association (APA). (2017). *Children, youth, families, and socioeconomic status.* Retrieved from www.apa.org/pi/ses/resources/publications/factsheet-cyf.pdf

Australian Bureau of Statistics (ABS). (2017). *2940.0 – census of population and housing: Details of overcount and undercount, Australia, 2016.* Retrieved from www.abs.gov.au/AUSSTATS/abs@.nsf/Lookup/2940.0Main+Features12016?OpenDocument

Australian Institute of Family Studies (AIFS). (2017). *Children in care (CFCA Resource Sheet-October 2017).* Canberra: AIFS. Retrieved from https://aifs.gov.au/cfca/publications/children-care

Australian Institute of Health and Welfare. (2017). *Child protection Australia 2015–2016 (Child Welfare Series No. 66).* Canberra: AIHW.

Beauchamp, T. (2014). *Young people transitioning from out-of-home care to adulthood.* Review of policy and program approaches in Australia and overseas. Parramatta, Australia: Uniting Care.

Becares, L., & Priest, N. (2015). Understanding the influence of race/ethnicity, gender, and class on inequalities in academic and non-academic outcomes among eighth-grade students: Findings from an intersectionality approach. *PLoS ONE, 10*(10), e0141363. Retrieved from https://doi.org/10.1371/journal.pone.0141363

Brooks, G., & Tarling, R. (2012). Boosting the reading levels and attitudes of young people who have offended: A review of the evidence and the lessons learnt from an evaluation of TextNow. *Youth Justice, 12*(3), 184–198. doi:10.1177/1473225412459836

Centers for Disease Control and Prevention, Division of Adolescent and School Health (CDC). (2009). *School connectedness: Strategies for increasing protective factors among youth.* Atlanta, GA: U.S. Department of Health and Human Services.

Chapman, M. J., & Mitchell, D. (2013). Mindfully valuing people now: An evaluation of introduction to mindfulness workshops for people with intellectual disabilities. *Mindfulness, 4*(2), 168–178.

Clark, H., & Unruh, D. (2010). Transition practices for adjudicated youth with E/BDs and related disabilities. *Behavioural Disorders, 36*(1), 43–51.

Clinks, J. M. (2014). *The young review*. Birmingham: Barrow Cadbury Trust. Retrieved from www.youngreview.org/sites/default/files/clinks_young-review_report_dec2014.pdf

Cumming, T., Marsh, R., & Higgins, K. (2018). *School connectedness for students with disabilities: From theory to evidence-based practice*. Melbourne, VIC, Australia: Routledge.

Cumming, T., Strnadová, I., & Dowse, L. (2014). At-risk youth in Australian schools and promising models of intervention. *International Journal of Special Education, 29*(3), 16–25.

Dowse, L., Baldry, E., & Snoyman, P. (2009). Disabling criminology: Conceptualizing the intersections of critical disability studies and critical criminology for people with mental health and cognitive disabilities in the criminal justice system. *Australian Journal of Human Rights, 15*(1), 29–46.

Dowse, L., Cumming, T., Strnadová, I., Lee, J. S., & Trofimovs, J. (2014). Young people with complex needs: Whose responsibility? *Research and Practice in Intellectual and Developmental Disabilities, 1*(2), 174–185. doi:10.1080/23297018.2014.953671

Gagnon, J. C., & Richards, C. (2008). *Making the right turn: A guide about improving transition outcomes of youth involved in the juvenile corrections system*. Washington, DC: National Collaborative on Workforce and Disability for Youth, Institute for Educational Leadership.

Gorski, P. (2008). The myth of the culture of poverty. *Educational Leadership, 65*(7), 32–36.

GOV.UK. (n.d.). *Foster carers*. Retrieved from https://www.gov.uk

Grigorenko, E. L., Macomber, D., Hart, L., Naples, A., Chapman, J., Geib, C. F., . . . Wagner, R. (2015). Academic achievement among juvenile detainees. *Journal of Learning Disabilities, 48*(4), 359–368. doi:10.1177/0022219413500991

Heffernan, K. (2010). Educating students in foster care. *Principal Leadership*, 19–21.

The IRIS Center. (2012). *Classroom diversity: An introduction to student differences*. Retrieved from https://iris.peabody.vanderbilt.edu/

Kohler, P. D., Gothberg, J. E., Fowler, C., & Coyle, J. (2016). *Taxonomy for transition programming 2.0: A model for planning, organizing, and evaluating transition education, services, and programs*. Western Michigan University. Retrieved from www.transitionta.org.

Lane, K. L., Menzies, H. M., Ennis, R. P., & Bezdek, J. (2013). School-wide systems to promote positive behaviours and facilitate instruction. *Journal of Curriculum and Instruction, 7*(1), 6–31.

Maddern, K. (2009). Reforms could be second best escape route for offenders. *The Times Educational Supplement, 4868*, 26.

McKellar, N., & Cowan, K. C. (2011, September). Supporting students in foster care. *Principal Leadership*, 12–16.

Mendes, P., Baidawi, S., & Snow, P. C. (2014). Young people transitioning from out-of-home care in Victoria: Strengthening support services for dual clients of child protection and youth justice. *Australian Social Work, 67*(1), 6–23. doi:10.1080/0312407X.2013.8531

Milson-Black, L. (2017). *Implementing significant change to provide a tiered approach for literacy and numeracy interventions*. SEPLA Special Education Conference, Sydney, NSW, Australia.

Ministry of Justice. (2017). *Youth justice statistics 2015/16 for England and Wales*. London: Ministry of Justice and Youth Justice Board for England and Wales. Retrieved from www.gov.uk/government/statistics/youth-justice-statistics-2015-to-2016

National Center for Mental Health Promotion and Youth Violence Prevention. (2010). *The role of schools in supporting children in foster care*. Washington, DC: American Institutes for Research.

National Working Group on Foster Care and Education. (2014). *Foster care and education: Tools and resources for improving the education success of students and youth in foster care*. Retrieved from www.ncjfcj.org/sites/default/files/NationalEducationBrochure.pdf

New South Wales Department of Education. (n.d.). *Wellbeing for schools* [Website]. Retrieved from www.det.nsw.edu.au/wellbeing/succeed/out-of-home-care

NZ Stats. (2017). *Crime and justice.* Retrieved from https://www.stats.govt.nz/topics/crime-and-justice

O'Neill, S. C., Strnadová, I., & Cumming, T. M. (2017). Systems barriers to community re-entry for incarcerated youths: A review. *Children and Youth Services Review.* doi:10.1016/j.childyouth.2017.05.025

Palmieri, L. E., & La Salle, T. P. (2016). Supporting students in foster care. *Psychology in the Schools, 54*(2), 117–126.

Regan, K. S., & Michaud, K. M. (2011). Best practices to support student behaviour. *Beyond Behaviour, 20*(2), 40–47.

Richards, L., Garratt, E., & Heath, A. F. (2016). *The childhood origins of social mobility: Socio-economic inequalities and changing opportunities.* London: Social Mobility Commission.

Senate Community Affairs Committee Secretariat. (2015). *Out of home care.* Canberra: Commonwealth of Australia.

Sedlak, A. J., & Bruce, C. (2017). *Survey of youth in residential placement: Youth characteristics and backgrounds.* SYRP Report. Rockville, MD, Westat.

Strnadová, I., O'Neill, S. C., & Cumming, T. (2017). A snapshot of education behind the fence: Possibilities and issues in engaging incarcerated youth in Australia. *International Journal of Educational Research.* doi:10.1016/j.ijer.2017.06.004

U.S. Department of Education. (2016). *Students in foster care* [Website]. Retrieved from www2.ed.gov/about/inits/ed/foster-care/index.html

U.S. Department of Health and Human Services. (2016). *Administration for children and families, administration on children, youth and families, children's bureau, preliminary estimates for FY 2015* as of June 2016 (23), p. 6.

U.S. Department of Justice. (2017). *OJJDP statistical briefing book.* [Online]. Retrieved from www.ojjdp.gov/ojstatbb/crime/JAR_Display.asp?ID=qa05260

United Nations. (2016). *World youth report.* New York, NY: United Nations.

Zetlin, A., MacLeod, E., & Kimm, C. (2012). Beginning teacher challenges instructing students who are in foster care. *Remedial and Special Education, 33*(1), 4–13.

6

AT-RISK STUDENTS

LGBT+

Introduction

The authors feel that this chapter must begin with a statement on terminology. There are many different accepted terms to describe sexual orientation, sex, and gender identity. What is acceptable is ultimately determined by the individuals and groups that are being described by said terms. While not exhaustive, Box 6.1 defines some of the more commonly used terms, with definitions taken from throughout the literature. It is not the intention of the authors to exclude or insult any individual or group of people; the acronym LGBT+ (lesbian, gay, bisexual, transsexual, plus other groups) is used throughout most of this chapter, as LGBT+ is the term used throughout the education literature, and the + is designed to acknowledge and show respect for the other groups that are not included in that abbreviated acronym.

BOX 6.1 DEFINITIONS

Androgynous: Having the characteristics or nature of both maleness and femaleness: neither specifically feminine or masculine.

Asexual: Experiences little to no sexual attraction to other people.

Bisexual: A man or woman who is romantically, sexually and/or emotionally attracted to people of either sex.

Bullying: Unwanted negative behaviour, verbal, psychological or physical, conducted by an individual or group against another person (or persons), and which is repeated over time. The definition includes relational bullying, cyberbullying, and identity-based bullying (such as homophobic bullying, racist bullying, and bullying of those with special educational needs).

Cisgender: People whose gender identity matches the sex that they were assigned at birth.

Gay: A man or woman who is romantically, sexually, and/or emotionally attracted to people of the same sex. Many gay men prefer to be called "gay" rather than homosexual. Many women who are gay prefer to be identified as "lesbian".

Gender identity: How a person identifies themselves in terms of gender.

Heterosexual: A person sexually attracted to people of the opposite sex.

Homophobic Bullying: Refers to bullying of any form that has the added dimension of being based on actual or perceived sexual orientation.

Intersex: An umbrella term used for a variety of conditions in which a person is born with a reproductive or sexual anatomy that does not fit the typical definition of the female or male sex. Although intersex individuals do not always identify as transgender or do not consider themselves to be covered by the transgender umbrella, many of the issues experienced by transgender people are common to intersex people.

Lesbian: A woman who is romantically, sexually and/or emotionally attracted to women.

LGBT+I: An acronym for lesbian, gay, bisexual, transgender, and intersex.

Non-binary: Identifies as neither male nor female

Pansexual: Sexual or romantic attraction is not restricted by sex assigned at birth, gender, or gender identity.

Queer: An umbrella term used to describe a sexual orientation, gender identity, or gender expression that does not conform to heteronormative society.

Safe space: Welcoming, supportive, and safe environment for lesbian, gay, bisexual, and transgender (LGBT+) students.

Sexual orientation: Sense of attraction to or sexual desire for individuals of the same sex, other sex, both, or neither.

Transgender: An inclusive term describing people whose gender identity or gender expression is different from the sex listed on their birth certificate (i.e., their assigned birth sex). People under the transgender umbrella may describe themselves using one or more of a wide variety of terms – including transgender. It is always best to be led by the individual's preferred adjective. The word "trans" is commonly used by transgender people, and it is acceptable to use this shortened term when referring to a person who identifies as transgender. Some transgender people who live in their preferred gender simply see themselves as a man or a woman rather than a trans man or a trans woman. Some transgender people may be under the care of doctors in undergoing hormone treatment to change their bodies; some undergo surgery as well. But not all transgender people can or will take those steps, and a transgender identity is not dependent upon medical procedures.

Schools are frequently heterosexual and homophobic environments, not conducive to the learning and emotional needs of LGBT+ students. The classroom has been described as the most homophobic of all institutions, full of ostracism and verbal and physical aggression aimed at LGBT+ students. The consequences of this are anxiety, depression, suicide, traumatic stress, absenteeism, lower educational aspirations, and lowered academic achievement. Schools often do not consider the needs of this vulnerable populations, and in some jurisdictions, schools are allowed to engage in discrimination if they are religiously affiliated (GLEN, 2016).

This chapter will outline the support needs of LGBT+ youth and how their academic, emotional, and behavioural needs can be met through evidence-based practices and a culturally responsive approach, as part of the multi-tiered culturally responsive system of support (MTCRSS). The majority of the necessary supports occur within the universal and tertiary levels, with broader support needed from legislative bodies.

LGBT+ students

Although statistics vary marginally by country, about 10% of the population has a diverse sexual orientation, sex, or gender identity (Australian Human Rights Commission, 2014; Center for Disease Control and Prevention, 2017). In addition to students who identify as LGBT+, an increasing number of students are living in same-sex couple families (Australian Human Rights Commission, 2014). Schools in the Anglosphere have only recently begun to recognise this significant population of students and address their unique needs. Prior to this, the LGBT+ student population was often ignored, or worse, persecuted.

It is important for LGBT+ student populations to be recognised throughout K-12 schooling. The most common age of LGBT+ identity is 12 years. The average age of coming out to at least one other person is 16. Young people are coming out at an earlier age, thus narrowing the gap between knowing and telling years. Trans youth typically realise their orientation identity before they leave primary school (GLEN, 2016).

The level of support provided by family, friends, and school determines how easy or difficult the coming out experience is for them. For most, it can be difficult and traumatic, as the young person may fear being isolated or rejected. For many young people, the gap of time between knowing and telling is made more challenging by the milestones that are simultaneously happening in their lives, such as school exams and planning to transition from school to further schooling or employment. Schools need to ensure that the school climate is safe and supportive for all students, including recognising the support needs of young people who are LGBT+.

Although more LGBT+ young people are coming out with the support of family, friends, community, and school, some may still experience many difficulties, especially when they are not supported. Being accepted and respected for who a person is as an individual is very important to the formation of a positive self-identity and quality of life (GLEN, 2016). The Australian Rights Commission (2014) reports that 80% of homophobic bullying occurs at school; 60% of LGBT+ students experience verbal homophobic abuse; 20% experience physical homophobic abuse. LGBT+ students who have experienced bullying or discrimination are more likely than their peers to avoid extracurricular activities, skip school, have lower grades, fail to plan for tertiary education, misuse substances, engage in risky sexual behaviour, experience risky sexual behaviours, experience depression, or have suicidal ideation/attempt suicide (Cornum, 2016; KidsHealth, 2015).

The negative school experiences of many LGBT+ young people puts them at risk of not achieving their full potential, low self-esteem, dropping out of school, mental health issues, and engaging in self-injurious behaviour (GLEN, 2016). This population of students also typically experiences a lack of school connectedness; only 20% of students felt that they felt that they belonged at school, but 44% felt that they received affirmation of their LGBT+ identity.

Legislation to protect LGBT+ students around the Anglosphere varies. In the US, less than half of the fifty states have laws to protect LGBT+ students (Human Rights Watch, 2016); eight states actually have laws that restrict teachers and staff from talking about LGBT+ issues at school. In the UK, *The Equality Act 2010* (legislation.gov.uk, 2010) provided LGBT+ people with the same legal protections as other groups who faced discrimination and mandated that public service providers like schools have to show how they are accessible and supportive of LGBT+ people. In Australia, the *Sex Discrimination Act 1984* was amended in 2013 to make discrimination on the basis of a person's sexual orientation, gender identity, and intersex status illegal (Australian Human Rights Commission, 2014).

Despite this legislation, a US study found that bullying, harassment, and aggression towards LGBT+ students still proliferates in schools (Human Rights Watch, 2016). High school students reported that in some cases, not only did teachers do nothing to stop the teasing, some even joined in. They also discovered that LGBT+ students lack teacher role models. This could be due to LGBT+ teachers fearing backlash from parents or employers if they were open about their orientation or identity.

Swanson and Gettinger (2016) reported on similar conditions in Australia. They discovered that LGBT+ students typically experience hostile school environments. They hear biased language, feel unsafe, are regularly harassed and are less likely to feel like a part of their school, compared to their peers. Results of their study also indicated that while teachers rated the importance of supporting LGBT+ students as high to very high, few of them were actually providing any support to those students. They identified a lack of knowledge related to how to support LGBT+ students, discomfort around LGBT+ issues, an unwillingness to provide support because of discriminatory attitudes towards LGBT+ students, and being unaware of the importance of intervening as barriers to the provision of support.

Taylor et al. (2016) surveyed K-12 teachers in Canada and discovered gaps between what teachers believe about LGBT+-inclusive education, their perceptions of school climate, and whether they practice LGBT+-inclusive education.

The gaps they identified included:

1 Most teachers perceived their schools as safe, yet many reported that LGBT+ students would not feel safe in their schools.
2 The majority of teachers believed that LGBT+ rights are human rights, but some did not approve of LGBT+-inclusive education.
3 The majority of teachers believed that LGBT+ rights are human rights, but some agreed that teachers should be able to opt out of LGBT+-inclusive education for religious reasons.
4 The majority of teachers believed that LGBT+ rights are human rights, but many do not talk about LGBT+ issues with students.
5 Most teachers approve of LGBT+-inclusive education, but fewer said they would be comfortable doing it, and fewer still are doing it.
6 Most teachers approve of LGBT+-inclusive education, but many feel that they would not be supported in practising it.

These gaps indicate a need for professional development for teachers and school leaders, and the establishment of school policy that specifically calls for supports and inclusive curricula. Anti-bullying policies that specifically mention LGBT+ students have been found to be significantly more effective than generic anti-bullying policies (GLEN, 2016; Kull, Greytak, Kosciw, & Villenas, 2016; Swanson & Gettinger, 2016; Taylor et al., 2016).

Vega, Crawford, and Van Pelt (2012) suggested that the blame for hostile and unsafe school cultures and climates lies with teachers and school leaders. They conducted a literature review and concluded that homophobia can take the form of silence, especially when teachers don't have the language to discuss sexualities. This silence sends the message that homophobia is acceptable. The literature showed that teachers and school staff often place the blame on LGBT+ students for the bullying they receive, and that teachers' heteronormative behaviour is related to the amount of support they receive. Vega et al. summarised that the core of these problems is that LGBT+ issues are not often covered in teacher preparation programs, and there is a lack of professional development for in-service teachers; thus, many teachers still hold negative beliefs about LGBT+ students and view sexuality as a private issue that doesn't belong in the classroom.

The literature indicates that although some progress is being made in legislation and policy to support LGBT+ students and provide them with safe and inclusive environments, there is still a long way to go, as bullying towards LGBT+ students is widespread internationally (Cornum, 2016). Homophobic and transphobic bullying is an obstacle to the right to education, which is one of the basic human rights set out in the United Nations Convention on the Rights of the Child (Cornum, 2016). It is clear from the present state of school experiences of LGBT+ students described in the literature that reforms must focus on legislation and policy that specifically protects young LGBT+ people, teacher professional learning, and improvement of school culture and climate.

Implications for practice

While there is much that schools can do to improve the social, emotional, and academic experiences of LGBT+ students, systemic changes need to happen at a governmental level first. Laws protecting LGBT+ students from bullying, harassment, and violence must be a priority, to provide departments of education and individual schools with guidance and a firm basis for their own policies to make schools safe and inclusive for LGBT+ students. The Human Rights Watch (2016) recommends that governments ensure that there are laws in place protecting people from bullying and harassment based on their sexual orientation and gender identity.

Non-discrimination laws must explicitly protect people from discrimination based on their sexual orientation and gender identity, particularly in education, employment, and public accommodation. In addition, outdated stigmatising laws that disadvantage LGBT+ students by prohibiting discussion of their issues in schools should be repealed, and instead laws should be enacted protecting students and staff from bullying and discrimination based on their sexual orientation and gender identity (Human Rights Watch, 2016).

On a global level, the United Nations Educational, Scientific, and Cultural Organization (UNESCO) is addressing homophobic and transphobic bullying in education by using a human rights-based approach that stresses that LGBT+ students have the same educational rights as their peers. This may go a long way in alerting policy makers to the fact that sexual orientation and gender identity are included in the Convention on the Rights of the Child and should be included in policy and school-based programs focused on addressing discrimination (Cornum, 2016).

School policies

When schools enact protective policies, LGBT+ students are more likely to feel safe, half as likely to be physically abused, and less likely to self-harm or attempt suicide (Australian Human Rights Commission, 2014). Education policy must specifically ban discrimination against LGBT+ students and teachers (Curwood & Ullman, 2014). Violence prevention and other school programs should recognise the existence of LGBT+ students and the challenges they face (Cornum, 2016).

School anti-bullying policies that specifically address homophobic and transphobic bullying are more effective than generic bullying policies and improve school safety for that population. Kull et al. (2016) found that when LGBT+I-specific policies were students were implemented, students were subject to less victimisation based on their sexual orientation and gender identity. Using an ecological perspective that acknowledges that bullying and harassment of LGBT+ students occurs within complex social and institutional systems can be effective for improving school climate.

Education policies on LGBT+ students also have significant effects on school climates, so it is important for state education sectors to take an anti-discriminatory safe and supportive schools approach to policy, including policies devoted to LGBT+ student issues. There is strong evidence that these policies and their implementation can promote better quality of life for this student population, as well as better life outcomes. However, policy is only a piece of the overall puzzle. The school environment needs to engage in other efforts to make schools safer for all students such as curricular inclusion and positive representation of LGBT+ people and topics, the establishment of Gay-Straight Alliances (GSAs), and staff support of LGBT+ students (Kull et al., 2016).

Preservice and professional development

The importance of including education about LGBT+ students in school leader, teacher, and counsellor preservice training cannot be understated, as a lack of knowledge is a reported barrier for providing support. School counsellors, in particular, play a large role in supporting LGBT+ students and educating school leaders and teachers about how they too can provide support. One of the roles of counsellor educators is to prepare preservice school counsellors to develop effective working relationships with school principals regarding LGBT+ topics in K-12 school settings. Research has shown that there is limited pedagogy in the area of LGBT+ students in school leadership and counsellor preparation programs (Beck, 2016). Counsellor educators should advise their students to discuss their roles as twenty-first-century school counsellors before beginning the conversation about LGBT+ students with principals. This will assist principals in gaining the understanding that counsellors are key preventative players and that their role is so much more than creating schedules. Preservice training programs need to recognise the complexity of advocating for and with LGBT+ students, beginning with trainees addressing their own biases and attitudes towards LGBT+ students. Preservice programs should also provide practitioners with experiential practice on how to facilitate self-reflective practices and support LGBT+ students.

Most of the challenges encountered by transgender people occur because of a lack of understanding that others have, particularly in the health and education sectors (GLEN, 2016). Current school leaders and personnel must receive professional development to familiarise them with LGBT+ students and their educational, psychological, and developmental needs and the issues they face (Aragon, Poteat, Espelage, & Koenig, 2012). School leadership teams must be supportive if teachers are to practice LGBT+-inclusive education, so it is important that training be provided to school leaders on the importance of system support for LGBT+-inclusive education. The training should focus on equipping school leaders to provide support, encouragement, and resources to facilitate teachers' inclusive practice (Taylor et al., 2016). The CDC (2017) recommends that staff also receive professional development on how to create safe and supportive school environments for all students (CDC, 2017). Swanson and Gettinger (2016) found that teachers who had received a high level of professional development engaged more frequently in supportive behaviours towards LGBT+ students, and professional development was found to contribute to an overall positive school climate and teacher's attitudes and self-efficacy in supporting LGBT+ students.

Curricula

Curriculum has the potential to affect the knowledge, beliefs, and experiences of all people, and as such should not be censored to remove reference to and education about LGBT+ people. Any national or state prescribed curriculum must include the histories, perspectives, and works of LGBT+ people, not just in health and physical education (HPE) classes but throughout the content areas (Australian Human Rights Commission, 2014). This is not to say it should not be included in HPE classes; HPE curricula should include issues pertinent to LGBT+ students, using appropriate language and terminology (CDC, 2017; Human Rights Watch, 2016). The curriculum should be assessed for inclusiveness of positive representation of LGBT+ individuals and society. Teachers can use positive representations from pop culture to help students become more aware and respecting of LGBT+ people (Aragon et al., 2012). LGBT+ content and insights must be part of the curriculum, if it is to be inclusive of all students (Curwood & Ullman, 2014).

Teachers cite fear of parental complaint as the most common barrier to including LGBT+ topics in their sexuality education instruction; however, research suggests that the majority of parents feel that the topic of homosexuality should be included in sexual health education (Curwood & Ullman, 2014). This highlights the importance of school leaders and teachers staying current on the current research literature, as it will help them speak to reluctant parents. Educators need to realise that offending socially conservative parents is not a valid excuse for violating human rights, and they wouldn't accept that reason for any other human right. Teachers should be prepared to adapt inclusive education principles to LGBT+ content (Taylor et al., 2016).

Supporting students in a multi-tiered culturally responsive system of support

Like their peers, LGBT+ students access the academic and behavioural supports provided within the MTCRSS, as described in previous chapters. The following sections, therefore, focus on the specific evidence-based practices and supports for this population. Educators are reminded that LGBT+ students have unique cultures in addition to their ethnic cultures, and the model prescribes that gay culture be included with the others. The practices and supports are grouped into tiers for the sake of uniformity but are focused more upon creating inclusive environments and counselling-based approaches than typical academic and behavioural approaches. LGBT+ students show great resilience when supports such as GSAs, supportive teachers, and anti-bullying policies are established at school. These supports have been shown to increase school attendance, self-efficacy, grade point averages, and school connectedness (Beck, 2016).

Tier 1 (universal) supports

The first priority at this tier is to create a climate of *empowerment*, where all students know that diversity is welcomed and respected. LGBT+I students should feel valued, safe, and supported (GLEN, 2016). School leaders and staff should address victimisation and create supportive school environments free from victimisation and homophobic bullying (Aragon et al., 2012). They should collaborate with parents of LGBT+ students to develop the school's code of conduct and anti-bullying policy. This policy should extend to staff; they should not be discriminated against in employment or promotions for their sexual orientation or gender identity.

The school should provide education and awareness-raising opportunities to staff and students to support *knowledge construction* and *reduce prejudice*. This should be aimed to broaden understanding and clarity on the distinction between the concepts of sexual orientation and gender identity. Respect for difference should be stressed, especially in the use of correct terminology and appropriate language. All students should also receive instruction to educate them about transgender people and the challenges they face. It is recommended that this is carried out as part of an integrated curriculum (GLEN, 2016).

Teachers should investigate and deal with all reports of bullying, keep accurate written records of any bullying incidents, and follow the school and education department's bullying policy. Students need to be confident that if they report bullying that it will be taken seriously and treated promptly. Vulnerable students may find it more difficult to report bullying. There should be a standard form students can use, and they should be able to report bullying anonymously. A dedicated school email that parents can use to report is also a good idea but must be monitored regularly.

Teachers have a large role in increasing LGBT+ students' feeling of belonging and connectedness to their school. They need to first examine their own attitudes toward LGBT+I students, to ensure that they are not contributing to a homophobic school climate by making casual homophobic remarks (Aragon et al., 2012). They then need to recognise that there are LGBT+ students and staff at their school and include them and their families in the language they use rather than ignoring their existence and making them feel invisible (GLEN, 2016). On the other hand, teachers should make no assumptions about students', staff members', and parents' sexual orientation or gender identity.

Teachers can use the MTCRSS model to create a culture of *empowerment* in their classrooms. Creating and implementing classroom rules that focus on respect is an important step in preventing bullying. Make it clear that bullying, teasing, name calling, and violence are not tolerated. Teachers and other school staff can make it clear that gay name calling, such as using gay-related expressions scornfully, such as one student telling another that his response in class was "gay," is unacceptable. As part of multicultural content integration, teachers use language that is inclusive of all people and immediately respond to anti- LGBT+ behaviour in order to let students know that transphobia and homophobia are not tolerated (GLSEN,

2016). Conversation about LGBT+ people should be incorporated into all subject areas as part of *multicultural content integration* (GLEN, 2016). All school staff should discover and use each student's preferred name and pronoun and make sure their peers use them also (KidsHealth, 2015). To *reduce prejudice* and *construct knowledge* among their colleagues, teachers can be a role model for other educators; they can discuss LGBT+ students and the issues they face with others, distribute information, advocate for professional development, and give a presentation to school staff (GLSEN, 2016).

School leaders should include policies that ensure that same-sex couples can date and attend school functions on the same terms as other student couples. Ensure that students can access facilities, express themselves, and participate in classes, sports, and extracurricular activities in accordance with their gender identity (Human Rights Watch, 2016). Schools are also encouraged to support LGBT+ students through collaboration with community-based healthcare providers who are experienced at supporting LGBT+ youth in accessing health services such as HIV/STD testing and counselling, and psychological services (CDC, 2017).

Policies must also take into consideration the needs of trans students. For example, schools should eliminate separating students by gender, or at least during school activities. If this is not possible, then trans students should be included in the group of their preferred gender identity. Single sex schools should avoid gender stereotyping when planning programs and offer diverse programs with a wide range of interests and aptitudes (GLEN, 2016). Trans students should be permitted to wear the school uniform consistent with their gender identity. Any accommodations that will be required should be worked out with the student and family. At minimum, a gender-neutral option should be provided. HPE should be structured so that trans students can participate fully and safely without any discrimination. Individual cases must be considered separately, particularly in regard to contact sports such as rugby, and with regard for player safety. Uniforms for PE should be the same as for school – students should be able to wear the uniform of their preferred gender. Gender neutral options may have to be considered for activities like swimming. The website www.transathlete.com provides advice on how to implement these and other initiatives.

Tier 2: secondary prevention for some

Schools should consider the creation of Gay-Straight Alliances (GSAs), which have the potential to provide safe spaces to buffer against negative outcomes for LGBT+ students (Aragon et al., 2012). Although they serve as an important resource and support, they sometimes face opposition from school administration. To be fully inclusive, supportive, and promoting of an *empowering school culture*, policy must ensure that GSAs can operate on the same terms as other student organisations (Human Rights Watch, 2016). Schools must work to *reduce prejudice* and allow this to happen. The CDC (2017) encourages schools to support the formation of GSAs and other student-organised school clubs because of their benefits to the staff and student body. For example, Swanson and Gettinger (2016) found that teachers who worked in schools with a GSA engaged more frequently in supportive behaviours towards LGBT+ students than teachers in schools without a GSA, and LGBT+ students in those schools felt more supported. This suggests that GSAs are associated with positive teacher attitudes and behaviours that facilitate their support of LGBT+ students. This is aligned with all five of the culturally responsive MTCRSS components.

Tier 3: tertiary prevention for a few

This tier comprises individualised supports, such as counselling and support for LGBT+ students. As such, this section will be focussed on supporting students who are "coming out" (a metaphor for LGBT+ people's self-disclosure of their sexual orientation or of their gender identity) and/or transitioning. As these supports are highly individualised, school staff are reminded to incorporate the five components of culturally responsive education into any interventions. It is especially important that any educator or counsellor providing these supports to have previously examined and eliminated their own biases and prejudices before attempting to support LGBT+ students.

Coming out

A student's privacy is to be respected at all times, particularly in regard to their sexual orientation or gender identity. "Outing" a student or exposing that they are LGBT+ without their permission can compromise their emotional and physical safety. If a student discloses their LGBT+ status, or comes out, to a teacher, counsellor, or other staff member, the individual can offer support but should not assume that he or she needs help. The best advice to the trusted person is to model acceptance, appreciate the student's courage, and above all – listen! Teachers should be prepared to refer the student to someone else if they cannot answer questions or offer the support the young person needs (GLSEN, 2016).

Schools should not engage with the student's parents about his or her coming out unless there is legitimate concern for the student's safety (GLSEN, 2016). If the school and students are accepting, and the family is not, there is a chance the student will come out at school but not at home. The school should consider the other aspects of the student's identity in regards to coming out, such as their culture, religion, or disability. Students should not be asked about their sexual orientation or their gender identity unless they volunteer such information themselves, and it should not be assumed that they are troubled by their identity or orientation (GLEN, 2016). If the student is questioning their LGBT+ identity, teachers can explain that they are there to support the student and assure the student that they can talk about anything confidentially, with the exception of anything indicating that their safety is at risk.

If a student comes out in a one-to-one situation to a counsellor, the counsellor can ask questions; for example:

- Do any of your friends know?
- Does your family know?
- How have things been since you have come out?
- Who or what has helped you in the coming out process?
- What positive or negative experiences have you had while coming out
- Are there any issues you would like to discuss?

(GLEN, 2016, p. 44)

Trans students

Although awareness and acceptance of LGBT+ individuals have grown in the last two decades, trans students are the most vulnerable members of this population and face high levels of stigmatisation and marginalisation. It is important that schools respond accurately and according to good practice for supporting young trans people. Firstly, there is no standard response; each person is different, and a school leader should take time to know the student, family, and context to find individualised support solutions.

When a student first discloses a desire to attend school in his or her preferred gender, the support of the student should be first and foremost when responding. A climate of acceptance and respect must be fostered in the school. It is extremely important to ensure that the correct gender, name, and pronoun are used to address transgender or intersex people. This denotes respect and increases the level of safety and inclusion they feel while at school.

A transition plan should be developed with the student and family and should be confidential to avoid bullying. School personnel should discuss with the student their choice of name and choice of pronoun, along with what should be used in written correspondence with the family. The name used at school (student's preferred name) doesn't need to be the same as the name on the official register.

Toilets and changing rooms should be set up in a way that students can access the rooms that correspond with their gender identity. Students should be consulted when transitioning on how they would like to have this happen, and this should be included in the transition plan. This typically causes the most debate, as other students and their families may feel uncomfortable with trans students using the facilities. This is typically due to an unfounded fear that the trans student may behave inappropriately, and since it is unfounded, it is not a valid reason to refuse access to the student. The discomfort should be addressed through education and initiatives to foster understanding as part of a school culture and climate that values all students and diversity and prevents transphobic bullying.

A transition plan should be constructed when a student expresses a wish to attend school in his or her preferred gender. The plan should be student-led and student-focused. A trusted and knowledgeable staff member should support the student in the creation of the plan. Where possible, parents/guardians should be involved. GLEN (2016) offers advice on specific details about each aspect of the transition that should be addressed by the plan, including a timeframe for when each aspect will take place and how the transition will be communicated to teachers and students to prevent transphobic bullying. An expert on transgender identity from an external organisation can be consulted.

GLEN (2016, p. 25) suggests the following elements be included:

1. How the plan relates to school policies and procedures.
2. How it will be related to the school community, in order to create and maintain a positive school climate.
3. Whether communication with parents/guardians of other students is necessary.
4. Date of transition, pronoun usage, and name.
5. Plan for usage of toilets and changing facilities.
6. Arrangements for name changes to be effective from the date of transition (attendance sheets, name plates on lockers, badges).
7. Staff education and training.
8. How to inform students – does the student want to disclose to some ahead of the transition?
9. Education of wider student community.
10. Uniforms.

If the student determines that changing schools is the best way to transition, then processes for record sharing and student support should be set out ahead of time.

Conclusion

LGBT+ students are a vulnerable population, as schools are often a hostile climate for them, with a majority of students reporting being teased and bullied. This understandably results in poor academic, behavioural, health, and post-school outcomes for these young people. Fortunately, it doesn't have to be the case. School leaders can work to produce an inclusive school climate and culture that facilitates feelings of belonging and school connectedness of all students. Implementing a multi-tiered culturally responsive system of support provides a framework to meet every student's needs, including the specific needs of this population.

References

Aragon, S. R., Poteat, V. P., Espelage, D. L., & Koenig, B. W. (2012). The influence of peer victimization on educational outcomes for LGBT and non-LGBT high school students. *Journal of LGBT Youth, 11*(1), 1–19.

Australian Human Rights Commission. (2014). *Face the facts: Lesbian, gay bisexual, trans, and intersex people*. Sydney, NSW, Australia: Australian Human Rights Commission. Retrieved from www.humanrights.gov.au/publications

Beck, M. J. (2016). Bolstering the preparation of school counsellor–principal teams for work with LGBT youth: Recommendations for preparation programs. *Journal of LGBT Issues in Counseling, 10*(1), 2–15.

Centres for Disease Control and Prevention. (2017). *LGBT youth*. [Online]. Retrieved from www.cdc.gov

Cornum, C. (2016). Preventing and addressing homophobic and transphobic bullying in education: A human rights–based approach using the United Nations convention on the rights of the child. *Journal of LGBT Youth, 13*(1–2), 6–17.

Curwood, S. J., & Ullman, J. (2014). Australian schools must promote LGBT-inclusive education. *The Conversation*. Retrieved from http://theconversation.com/australian-schools-must-promote-lgbt-inclusive-education-23260

Gay and Lesbian Equality Network. (GLEN). (2016). *'Being LGBT in school' A resource for post-primary schools to prevent homophobic and transphobic bullying and support LGBT students*. Retrieved from www.education.ie/en/Publications/Education-Reports/Being-LGBT-in-School.pdf

GLSEN. (2016). *The safe space kit: Guide to being an ally to LGBT students*. New York, NY: GLSEN.

Human Rights Watch. (2016). *'Like walking through a hailstorm' Discrimination against LGBT youth in US schools*. Retrieved from www.hrw.org/report/2016/12/07/walking-through-hailstorm/discrimination-against-LGBT-youth-us-schools

KidsHealth. (2015). *Connecting with LGBT teens* [Website]. Retrieved from http://kidshealth.org/en/parents/LGBT-students.html

Kull, R. M., Greytak, E. A., Kosciw, J. G., & Villenas, C. (2016). Effectiveness of school district antibullying policies in improving LGBT youths' school climate. *Psychology of Sexual Orientation and Gender Diversity, 3*(4), 407–415.

Legislation.gov.uk. (2010). *Equality Act 2010*. [Online]. Retrieved from www.legislation.gov.uk/ukpga/2010/15/contents

Swanson, K., & Gettinger, M. (2016). Teachers' knowledge, attitudes, and supportive behaviours toward LGBT students: Relationship to gay-straight alliances, antibullying policy, and teacher training. *Journal of LGBT Youth, 13*(4), 326–351.

Taylor, C. G., Meyer, E. J., Peter, T., Ristock, J., Short, D., & Campbell, C. (2016). Gaps between beliefs, perceptions, and practices: The Every Teacher Project on LGBTQ-inclusive education in Canadian schools, *Journal of LGBT Youth, 13*(1–2), 112–140. doi: 10.1080/19361653.2015.1087929

Vega, S., Crawford, H. G., & Van Pelt, J. L. (2012). Safe schools for LGBTI students: How do teachers view their role in promoting safe schools? *Equity & Excellence in Education, 45*(2), 250–260.

7

DEVELOPING A CULTURALLY COMPETENT SCHOOL CLIMATE

Introduction

Schools are charged with ensuring that students succeed both academically and behaviourally. In order to support the social-emotional learning of students, a positive and caring school climate is necessary. It can be extremely difficult to make systematic changes in school climate as, at times, there are systems in effect that compete or do not integrate with these reforms. These variables can include lack of support from administration, lack of appropriate professional development, lack of resources, and lack of individualised supports for schools, teacher, and students (Freeman, Sugai, Simonsen, & Everett, 2017). It is vital that schools ensure that the school climate incorporates a culturally relevant framework, as this will ensure that the school climate is positive and caring for all students.

School climate has been a recognised construct for over 100 years (Wang & Degol, 2016). Until the past few decades, though, the characteristics of school climate were too simplistic. It is now understood to be multidimensional, incorporating four areas: (a) academic, (b) community, (c) safety, and (d) institutional environment (Wang & Degol, 2016). While there is not a generally agreed-upon definition of school climate, there are many commonalities among the terms used to describe the concept (Cohen, McCabe, Michelli, & Pickeral, 2009). For the purpose of this chapter, the National School Climate Council definition will be used. The National School Climate Council (NSCC) of the United States defines school climate as:

> the quality and character of school life. School climate is based on patterns of students', parents' and school personnel's experience of school life; it also reflects norms, goals, values, interpersonal relationships, teaching and learning practices, and organisational structures. A sustainable, positive school climate

> fosters youth development and learning necessary for a productive, contributory, and satisfying life in a democratic society.
>
> *(NSCC, 2010)*

The NSCC (2010) further stated that in a positive school climate the accepted norms, values, and expectations ensure that the teachers, staff, and students have feelings of safety in many areas (e.g., social-emotional and physical well-being). In a positive school climate, the stakeholders are engaged and respected. Stakeholders are engaged through their participation in school processes, such as developing and contributing to the school vision and how the school runs.

Research has shown that a positive school climate can have significant positive effects on the academic and behavioural outcomes of students. Schools with consistently high standards have shown greater growth for students in the areas of math and science (Zullig, Huebner, & Patton, 2011). Elementary school students have higher standardised test scores when their teachers set high but reachable goals for them and show students that they believe they will reach them (Kim & Kim, 2013). Wang and Degol (2016) conducted a review of school climate research and found that student achievement in schools that maintained high academic standards, strong school leadership, set high and attainable goals, and demonstrated strong commitment to students was higher than that of students who attended schools that did not incorporate these ideals.

In addition to academic outcomes, mental health and behavioural outcomes are also significantly impacted by the components of a positive school climate. Some of the benefits of a positive school climate include: (a) fewer discipline problems (Thapa, Cohen, Guffey, & Higgins-D'Alessandro, 2013), (b) a reduction in suspension rates (Gregory, Cornell, & Fan, 2011), (c) reduced rates of aggressive and disruptive behaviours (Gregory et al., 2010; Kaplan & Seginer, 2015; Wang, 2009), (d) a decrease in bullying behaviours (Bradshaw et al., 2009; Meyer-Adams & Conner, 2008), and (e) an increase in appropriate behaviours from students who were previously displaying difficulty in that area. The research supports that a positive school climate has a positive impact on students' academic and behavioural success. Cultural responsiveness is crucial if a school climate is to be supportive of all staff and students. This chapter outlines the importance of school climate as the core of the universal tier in the multi-tiered culturally responsive system of support (MTCRSS) model.

Dimensions of school climate

The NSCC has identified four essential dimensions of school climate. The dimensions must be built in such a way to support the academic and social-emotional needs of all students. These dimensions must first be assessed (e.g., The School Climate Survey). Once the climate has been assessed, school leaders can identify goals to ensure that the school setting eventually includes all of the dimensions.

These types of school-wide changes cannot occur without strong professional development for faculty and school leaders. Professional development that is consistent and evidence-based will support the school community to more effectively adopt the necessary changes (as identified through the assessment). School leadership is crucial –- leaders must be committed to these types of teaching and learning initiatives. School leaders must be able to clearly and effectively communicate a shared vision to the faculty and staff of the school. They must also be accessible and honour the work of the faculty and staff; this will foster faculty and staff buy-in.

Teaching and learning

The teaching and learning dimension is constructed of four characteristics: quality of instruction, social, emotional, and ethical learning, professional development, and leadership. The instructional setting of a school must include: (a) high expectations for all students, (b) academic supports for students who need them, (c) high levels of student engagement, (d) effective use of praise and reward, (e) a variety of teaching methods, and (f) value for successes other than traditional academic (e.g., creativity and artistic ability). Another important aspect of teaching and learning is ensuring that social, emotional, and ethical learning are included in the curriculum. This type of curriculum provides students with the socioemotional competencies and ethical dispositions necessary for them to become successful adults.

Community

The community dimension consists of four sub-dimensions: quality interpersonal relationships, connectedness, respect for diversity, and community partnerships. This dimension focuses on the relations within, between, and among school stakeholders. In order to have quality interpersonal relationships among school faculty and staff, there must be trust, respect, caring, and support. When there are strong relationships on a campus, the school will be better suited to meet the needs of students. An important piece of community is ensuring that students feel connected to the school. This connectedness piece includes students and faculty feeling bonded and attached to the school (Wang & Degol, 2016). Students and faculty who feel connected regard themselves as a fundamental part of the school.

Because of the great diversity in both our schools and globally (as the world becomes smaller), respect for diversity must be an integral part of a positive school climate. Respect for diversity requires that the school exhibit and teach cultural awareness, appreciation for those who are different, and how to be respectful to all. It is important that schools not only teach but model these skills for students. These skills can be modelled for students through community partnerships.

Having strong community partners, which includes parents and other stakeholders, allows the school to be an integral part of the community. Schools can have parents and community members provide professional development for staff and faculty on the diverse populations served by the school. Family involvement is a key component of community partnerships, as parents and carers also need to feel that they are seen as important to the school setting.

Safety

The safety dimension includes not only physical safety but also social-emotional safety. For this reason, rules and norms are important aspects of safety. School faculty and staff need to model and teach the school rules and support students in understanding the norms of how to interact and connect with others. When students are taught social and school behavioural norms, they are better able to build relationships with shared understandings. To promote the acquisition of social and behavioural skills, students should be in included in the development of the classroom level rules and norms. This will provide them with a sense of ownership and stronger understanding of the expectations.

The creation of a positive school climate requires school leaders to consider the social-emotional and physical safety of students and staff. Schools must address issues related to bullying, attitudes towards individual differences, and conflict resolution. It is also important that schools have caring and supportive faculty and staff and adequate counselling services, including trauma-informed practices. These create an environment that allows students to express their thoughts and feelings without fear of reprisal or bullying.

The physical safety dimension involves making the school a place that is free from violence, aggression, and victimisation (Wang & Degol, 2016). In a positive school climate, students feel that they are physically safe. Schools leaders can accomplish this by implementing evidence-based practices, such as: (a) positive behavioural intervention and supports, (b) clearly communicated rules, (c) consistent responses to inappropriate behaviour, and (d) effective classroom management techniques.

Institutional environment

The physical environment of the school is a major component of how people within the school experience the setting. A school that is well maintained by the faculty, staff, and students demonstrates the pride the school community has in the setting. It is important that enough resources are allocated for the school to have appropriate lighting, temperature, and sound control. Educational authorities need to ensure that there are similar resources (e.g., technology, curriculum, supplies) at all of their sites to ensure equity across schools, regardless of neighbourhood. Inequitable resources can lead to students at the less-funded sites having diminished feelings of self-worth. Schools must also ensure that the environment is physically accessible to all students and staff.

Supporting students in a multi-tiered culturally responsive system of support

School climate affects all students; therefore, it is a component of the universal tier of support in the MTCRSS model. Its main function is to provide an **empowering**

school culture. In order to ensure that a school climate is supporting the entire school community, all three tiers of the model need to incorporate attributes that are supportive of the needs of all staff and students, but the core business of propagating a positive school climate takes place at Tier 1, the universal tier. As school climate is reflective of the individuals who are part of the school community, climates will vary from school to school, based on the population of each.

Many attributes of a positive school climate are also included in the Positive Behaviour Interventions and Supports (PBIS) model. To adopt a positive school climate for all students, the school leadership team conducts an initial assessment to determine the strengths of the current school climate, along with areas that need improvement. This can be accomplished by using a school climate survey, along with an additional assessment of the student demographics of the school. This will assist the school faculty in determining any potential cultural mismatches between identified school norms and students' culture. These assessments must be done prior to adopting any universal expectations and behaviours. A culturally relevant practice checklist can be used in conjunction with the assessment results to inform the discussion around school behavioural expectations.

To meet the needs of students from different cultural backgrounds, educators need to include **equity pedagogy** for all students (Banks, 2016). Important aspects of **equity pedagogy** for students from diverse backgrounds are belonging, membership, and acceptance for all students. A foundational way to put this into practice is to create a community where all children have access to and participate in the general education classroom. The basic philosophy behind this community is that participation in the classroom is the norm; students do not have to earn their right to be placed in a classroom based on behaviour or academic expectations (McIntosh, Moniz, Craft, Golby, & Steinwand-Deschambeault, 2014). This will require educators to use management styles and instructional design which accommodate a range of student learning and behavioural differences (Petrie, 2014). In the course of doing this, teachers should be mindful that they are **integrating culturally relevant content**. Teachers must also acknowledge and support different communication styles by incorporating these into learning activities to promote a sense of community and acceptance, thereby **reducing prejudice** (Kaplan Toren & Seginer, 2015).

Implementing school climate reform

School leaders should work with their community in ensure there is a positive school climate. The National School Climate Center (2010) has suggested a five-step process to reform school climate.

Preparation and planning

Preparation and planning are vital for the success of the implementation plan. In order to begin the planning, a school leadership team needs to be developed. It is important to include members from all stakeholder groups in the planning, such as teachers and other school staff, students, families, and the wider community. This will allow for **knowledge construction**, producing new understandings and knowledge that exceeds something that anyone alone could achieve. It also permits the team to consider the impact of any decisions on the entire school community. Some of the things that need to be discussed within the team are how to cultivate and ensure buy-in from school and community members (Bryk, Sebring, Allensworth, Luppescu, & Easton, 2010). The leadership team will need to have discussions about what they believe should be the components of the climate at the school. The team will define the school climate standards for the school and ensure integration between teaching and learning, safety, instructional environment, and community (Jennings & Greenberg, 2009). Research shows that this type of collaboration around a shared vision will increase the likelihood that everyone will buy into and support the reform initiative moving forward. This discussion should then be shared with the community at large for feedback. A goal of this leadership group will also be to raise awareness of the school climate dimensions, standards, and research and to lead to agreement by all the school and community stakeholders. In order to ensure that this work is successful, it will need to be appropriately resourced. Once the vision for the new school climate has been identified and agreed upon, the next step will be to conduct a gap analysis.

Assess current climate

The next step is to assess the current climate and identify gaps between where the school site is and where the community would like it to be. All dimensions of school climate (teaching and learning, safety, instructional environment, community) should be assessed (Cohen et al., 2009). Data should be gathered from all school stakeholders. Some ways to assess school climate will be structured observations, focus groups with students, teachers, parents, and community, interviews, town halls, action research, and surveys. An example of an assessment is the Center for Social and Emotional Education's (CSEE) *Comprehensive School Climate Inventory* (NSCC, 2015). The school leadership team decides what assessments will be conducted and how the data will be analysed. The end goal of the assessment will be to identify the strengths, areas of improvement, and needs for school climate reform. This type of assessment will be continual to ensure that the school climate is consistently assessed and improved using research-based tools. The findings of these data should be shared with all school stakeholders (faculty, staff, students, family, and community).

Develop an action plan

Once the data have been collected, the leadership team analyses the data to determine what the areas of commonality and differences between the stakeholders are.

This analysis should be shared with community stakeholders for input. From this information, the leadership team will identify, rank, and prioritise the goals. Once the goals have been identified, the leadership team will develop the action plan. The plan states the goal, the strategies that will be used to meet the goal, how progress towards the goal will be measured, and who will be the lead person to manage the implementation and evaluation of the plan. The action plan identifies the specific intended outcomes and the impacts of school climate reform and effective assessment measures.

Implementation of the action plan

From the developed action plan, the leadership team will ensure that there are enough resources to implement the action plan. The leadership team will identify and coordinate the implementation of evidence-based pedagogic and systemic efforts which will promote students' social, emotional, and academic skills and improve the school climate through working toward a safe, caring, and responsive school community. A focus of the leadership team should remain on shared leadership and diverse perspectives throughout this process. That will provide the needed sustainability for the school climate reform. Consistent positive relationships among students, among adults, and between students and adults in the school and community are vital for a positive school climate.

The leadership team ensure that the instructional and school-wide efforts are implemented with fidelity and are continually monitored. This will include ongoing reflection to learn from successes and challenges through the process. During the implementation process, policies need to be created that will allocate resources to effectively implement the school climate assessments, data analysis, and improvement. The leadership team should identify ways for students to participate in the leadership of the climate reform, as their contributions will assist with the buy-in of the community. Additionally, the leadership team will need to allocate resources which allow for continual professional development around school climate knowledge and skills throughout the faculty, staff, and professional learning communities (Payne, 2009).

Re-evaluation and next phase development

As with any school reform, re-evaluation is a vital component. The leadership team should identify assessment points which will allow for the identification of school climate strengths and challenges. This continual monitoring will allow for the team to understand what has changed and how it has changed. This will determine what has been the most instrumental and what has gotten in the way of improving the school climate at the school site. At each re-evaluation stage, a new plan of action should be developed so that the school climate is always being assessed and improving.

Conclusion

As schools move towards a multi-tiered system of support for behaviour and academic needs, a positive school climate must be in place. While school climate reform is a universal system of support, faculty must use and model the school behavioural expectations and classroom norms while supporting students who move through the tiers due to academic or behavioural concerns. School climate impacts how students are able to engage and learn in their environment. Steps for implementing school climate reform will assist teams in ensuring that all students feel welcomed and cared about in their school and classroom.

References

Banks, J. A. (2016). *Cultural diversity and education* (6th ed.). New York, NY: Routledge.

Bradshaw, C. P., Sawyer, A. L., & O'Brennan, L. M. (2009). A social disorganization perspective on bullying-related attitudes and behaviors: The influence of school context. *American Journal of Community Psychology, 43*, 204–220.

Bryk, A. S., Sebring, P. B., Allensworth, E., Luppescu, S., & Easton, J. Q. (2010). *Organizing schools for improvement: Lessons from Chicago*. Chicago: University of Chicago Press.

Cohen, J., McCabe, E. M., Michelli, N. M., & Pickeral, T. (2009). School climate: Research, policy, teacher education and practice. *Teachers College Record, 111*(1), 180–213.

Freeman, J., Sugai, G., Simonsen, B., & Everett, S. (2017). MTSS coaching: Bridging knowing to doing. *Theory into Practice, 56*(1), 29–37.

Gregory, A., Cornell, D., & Fan, X. (2011). The relationship of school structure and support to suspension rates for Black and White high school students. *American Educational Research Journal, 48*, 904–934. doi:10.3102/0002831211398531

Gregory, A., Cornell, D., Fan, X., Sheras, P. L., Shih, T., & Huang, F. (2010). Authoritative school discipline: High school practices associated with lower student bullying and victimization. *Journal of Educational Psychology, 102*, 483–496. doi:10.1037/a0018562

Jennings, P. A., & Greenberg, M. T. (2009). The pro-social classroom: Teacher social and emotional competence in relation to student and classroom outcomes. *Review of Educational Research, 79*(1), 491–525.

Kaplan Toren, N., & Seginer, R. (2015). Classroom climate, parental educational involvement, and student school functioning in early adolescence: A longitudinal study. *Social Psychology of Education, 18*, 811–827.

Kim, D. H., & Kim, J., H. (2013). Social relations and school life satisfaction in South Korea. *Social Indicator Research, 112*, 105–127. doi:10.1007/s11205-012-0042-8

McIntosh, K., Moniz, C., Craft, C. B., Golby, R., & Steinwand-Deschambeault, T. (2014). Implementing school-wide positive behavioural interventions and supports to better meet the needs of indigenous students. *Canadian Journal of School Psychology, 29*(3), 236–257.

Meyer-Adams, N., & Conner, B. T. (2008). School violence: Bullying behaviors and the psychosocial school environment in middle schools. *Children & Schools, 30*(4), 211–221.

National School Climate Center (NSCC). (2010). *A five stage school climate improvement process: Research support and information about best practices that support the tasks/challenges that define each of the five SC improvement stages*. Retrieved from www.schoolclimate.org/themes/schoolclimate/assets/pdf/stages-tasks-and-challenges/ResearchSupport-FiveStages.pdf

National School Climate Center (NSCC). (2015). *The comprehensive school climate inventory*. Retrieved from www.frsu38.org/userfiles/15/my%20files/wes%20full%20climate%20 results.pdf?id=3488

Payne, A. A. (2009). Do predictors of the implementation quality of school prevention programs differ by program type? *Prevention Science, 10,* 151–167.

Petrie, K. (2014). The relationship between school climate and student bullying. *TEACH Journal of Christian Education, 8*(1), 25–35.

Thapa, A., Cohen, J., Guffey, S., & Higgins-D'Alessandro, A. (2013). A review of school climate research. *Review of Educational Research, 83,* 357–385. doi:10.3102/0034654313483907Wang, M. (2009). School climate support for behavioral and psychological adjustment: Testing the mediating effect of social competence. *School Psychology Quarterly, 24,* 240–251. doi:10.1037/a0017999Wang, M., & Degol, J. L. (2016). School climate: A review of the construct, measurement, and impact on student outcomes. *Educational Psychology Review, 28,* 315–352. doi:10.1007/s10648-015-9319-1Zullig, K. J., Huebner, E. S., & Patton, J. M. (2011). Relationships among school climate domains and school satisfaction. *Psychology in the Schools, 48,* 133–145.

8
CONCLUSION

There has been an increased focus on supporting students at risk in today's schools to improve their level of connectedness with their schools, teachers, peers, and academics, thereby improving their post-school outcomes (Cumming, Marsh, & Higgins, 2018). The research shows that achieving this is more effective when using a school-wide multi-tiered approach to both behaviour management and academics (Cumming et al., 2018). The authors of this book have suggested that this approach be taken a step further and include the elements of cultural responsiveness in order to ensure that school is a totally inclusive, supportive environment. Never has this been more crucial than the present, where we are greeted with alarming news of increasing school violence on an almost daily basis.

While culturally responsive pedagogy (CRP) has its roots in supporting students of colour, we have expanded this to include other marginalised populations, as ethnicity alone does not determine one's culture. Many students overlap and can be identified in several of the groups mentioned in this volume; this is more reason for schools to establish practices that are inclusive of ALL students. This includes groups of students who were not specifically addressed in this volume, such as the "square pegs", or misfits, who struggle to fit into school academic and/or social environments. The proposed multi-tiered culturally responsive system of support (MTCRSS) model allows for students to move up and down and left and right between the three tiers of both academic and social/behavioural support, with concurrent multicultural content integration, knowledge construction, prejudice reduction, and equity pedagogy, all delivered within an empowering school culture.

The three tiers of the model each serve a specific purpose, but the importance of the universal tier cannot be overstated. It includes the school climate, which is the grounding for the school's culture (Zullig, Huebner, & Patton, 2011). When the suggestions in this tier are implemented effectively, students feel safe and connected to their school. Everyone in the school community has a voice – students, families, teachers, staff, and the wider community. Teams including these groups are developed to plan and monitor school improvement initiatives, as well as to address students at risk for academic and behavioural issues. These teams ensure that there is an awareness of what is going on in and around the school, and any identified issues, such as bullying, are addressed immediately and efficiently, supporting both the bully and the student being bullied. Above all else, a positive school climate incorporates the tenets of an empowering school culture, where all students experience academic and social equality.

The academic side of the universal tier includes careful consideration of what is included in the curriculum. For example, history curricula should include the history of all groups, factoring in the history of groups that are often overlooked, such as students with disabilities and LGBT+ students (Curwood & Ullman, 2014). In order to be fully inclusive and culturally responsive, schools must consider how students learn English, trauma-informed practice, and the possibility of mismatches between students' individual cultures and the typical Western school culture. Adjustments can be made pedagogically to account for these considerations and ensure that all students are receiving every opportunity to succeed academically.

When students' academic, behavioural, and socioemotional needs are not adequately met through the supports provided in the universal tier, they may be provided with more focused intervention and supports in the second tier. The supports in this tier are evidence-based and more tailored to specific groups of students. Examples provided in this book include Gay-Straight Alliances, small group instruction, and social skills instruction. When implemented via the MTCRSS, these practices will employ content integration, an equity pedagogy, to support students' construction of knowledge. These will, in turn, serve to empower students from all groups and reduce prejudice.

There is typically a small percentage of students who require more intensive individualised behavioural and/or academic supports. Many times, these support needs are reflective of a disability, mental health issue, or chronic illness (Stobier & Gettinger, 2016). In most cases, interventions and supports are provided by an expert, such as a special education teacher or counsellor. When planning supports at this tier, the student and family should always have a voice in planning supports at this tier, and all interventions and supports should incorporate the five tenets of cultural responsiveness. This is particularly important when conducting a functional behavioural assessment, as misbehaviour is a subjective construct.

The proposed MTCRSS is designed to be comprehensive in meeting the needs of all students, using a continuous cycle of assessment and provision of support. Students are individuals with their own cultures, and in order to feel connected to their schools and experience successful outcomes, they need to feel that their unique attributes are recognised and respected and their needs met. The incorporation of cultural responsiveness to existing MTSS aims to provide a framework to guide schools in providing a safe and supportive environment for all students.

Future directions

The evidence base supporting multi-systemic systems of support is dependent upon fidelity of implementation, which involves a continuous cycle of assessment (OSEP Technical Assistance Center on Positive Behavioral Interventions and Supports, 2015). Therefore, it is recommended that future research focus on assessing the MTCRSS. This can be accomplished by adding items to fidelity assessments to measure the integration of the five components of cultural responsiveness (equity pedagogy, prejudice reduction, knowledge construction, content integration, and empowerment) into the three-tiered model.

It is predicted that the effectiveness of the model will be dependent upon its implementation as a fully integrated system from the start. Cultural responsiveness is an organic component of each tier of the model, and not to be considered an add-on or afterthought. When implemented with fidelity, it is expected that the multi-tiered culturally responsive system of support will improve the school experience of all students by providing each with the support they need to be successful.

References

Cumming, T., Marsh, R., & Higgins, K. (2018). *School connectedness for students with disabilities: From theory to evidence-based practice*. Melbourne, VIC, Australia: Routledge.

Curwood, S. J., & Ullman, J. (2014). Australian schools must promote LGBT-inclusive education. *The Conversation*. Retrieved from http://theconversation.com/australian-schools-must-promote-lgbt-inclusive-education-23260

OSEP Technical Assistance Center on Positive Behavioral Interventions and Supports. (2015, October). *Positive Behavioral Interventions and Supports (PBIS) implementation blueprint: Part 1 – foundations and supporting information*. Eugene, OR: University of Oregon. Retrieved from www.pbis.org

Stobier, K. C., & Gettinger, M. (2016). Multi-tiered systems of support and evidence-based practices. In S. R. Jimerson, M. K. Burns, & A. M. VanDerHeyden (Eds.), *Handbook of response to intervention* (pp. 121–141). New York, NY: Springer Publishing.

Zullig, K. J., Huebner, E. S., & Patton, J. M. (2011). Relationships among school climate domains and school satisfaction. *Psychology in the Schools, 48*, 133–145.

INDEX

Note: Page numbers in *italic* indicate a figure and page numbers in **bold** indicate a table on the corresponding page.

applied behaviour analysis (ABA) 12–14
at-risk students 1, 29, 44, 58, 61–62, 75, 101–103; cultural perspectives of 51–55; and implications for practice 67–68, 83–85; indigenous students, 33–34; language learners 29–31; LGBT+ 78–82, 90; migrant children 31–32; MTCRSS support for 36–40, 55–57, 68–74, 85–90; refugee students 32–33; students in out-of-home care 65–67, **65**; students involved with the juvenile justice system 64–65; students with chronic illness 50–51; students with disabilities 44–46, **46**; students with low socioeconomic status 62–64; students with mental health issues 46–50, **47**
Australia: chronic illness in 50; cultural perspectives in 53; disabilities in 44–46, **46**; ELLs in 30–31; indigenous students in 33, 61; juvenile justice system in 64; LGBT+ students in 80–81; mental health issues in 46–47; migrant children in 32; young people of color in 61; SES in 62

Banks, J. A. 6–7, 18, 20
basic interpersonal communication skills (BICS) 36
behaviourist theory 34, 36
Bianco, M. 20
bullying 93, 95, 102; LGBT+ students and 1, 78–79, 81–83, 86, 89–90; MTCRSS and 22, 55; PBIS and 6

chronic illness 44,50–51, 58, 102; cultural perspectives of 51–55; support for students with 55–57
classroom setting *see* setting
climate *see* school climate
cognitive/academic language proficiency (CALP) 36
coming out 80, 88–89
common underlying proficiency theory 35–36
communication: common underlying proficiency theory and 36; cultural differences and 54; home-school 14, 39; language acquisition and 35; MTCRSS and 69, 71; and students involved with the juvenile justice system 64; teacher-student 1; trans students and 90
community 101–102; CRP and 18; cultural perceptions and 53; indigenous culture and 36; juvenile justice system and 64–65, 74; MTCRSS and 21, 69; MTSS and 15; RtI and 14; school climate and 92, 94–98; SES and 62–63

constructionism learning theory 12, 18, 53
content integration 7, 101–103; and LGBT+ students 86–87; MTCRSS and 71–72, 22, 37, 55; UDL and 19
culturally responsive education (CRE) 6–10, 17–19, 88
culturally responsive pedagogy (CRP) 9, 17–19, 20, 101
curricula 102; indigenous students and 34; LGBT+ students and 82, 84–86; MTCRSS and 22–24, 37–38, 55–56, 68, 72; multicultural content integration and 7; refugee students and 33; RtI and 2–3; school climate and 94–95; universal design for learning and 19

disabilities 1, 44–46, **46**, 58, 61–65, 102; assessing for 9; coming out and 88; cultural perspectives of 51–55; ELLs and 30; migrant children and 31; MTCRSS and 25, 40; support for students with 55–57
discipline 1, 5, 16, 24, 66, 93
diversity 1, 7, 18, 37, 86, 89, 94

empowering school culture 8–9, 101–102; CRP and 18; MTCRSS and 21, 37, 68, 87
English language learners (ELLs) 29–32, 37; *see also* second language acquisition
environment *see* institutional environment; school climate; setting
equality 8, 102
equity pedagogy 101–103; culturally responsive education and 7–8, 18–19; MTCRSS and *13*, 22, 37–38, 40, 55–57, 69, 71–73; school climate and 96
ethnicity 8, 68, 101
extracurricular activities 18, 21, 69, 81, 87

families 102; and at-risk students 1; and cultural perspectives on disability and illness 52–55; of ELLs 30; interactionist theory and 35; and the juvenile justice system 64; and LGBT+ students 80, 86–89; and low socioeconomic backgrounds 62–63; of PBIS and 4, 14; of migrant children 31–32; MTCRSS and 10, 22, 24, 39–40, 56–57, 70–74; and out-of-home care 65–67, **65**; RtI and 15; school climate and 94, 97; of students with anxiety disorders 48; of students with chronic illness 50–51; of students with disabilities 46; *see also* parents

Gagnon, J. C. 1
Gay and Lesbian Equality Network (GLEN) 90
Gettinger *see* Swanson
Groce, N. 51, 53
GSA 88

Harris *see* Bianco
health care 15, 51, 54–55, 63, 65
Horner *see* Sugai

immigration *see* migrant children
implementation science 12, 15–17
indigenous students 33–34, 36–37, 52, 61, 64
individual education program (IEP) 40, 46
individual learning plan (ILP) 46
inequality 9, 63
innatist theory 34–36
institutional environment 92, 95
interactionist theory 35–36
Internet 62–63

juvenile justice system 64–65, 67–69, 73–75

knowledge construction 101, 103; culturally responsive education and 7–8; LGBT+ students and 86; MTCRSS and *13*, 22, 37, 39, 55, 69, 71–72; school climate and 97

language learners 29; *see also* English language learners (ELLs)
LaSalle *see* Palmieri
LGBT+ students 1, 78–82, 90, 102; MTCRSS support for 85–90; and schools 83–85

mental health issues 46–47, 58; anxiety disorders 47–48; attention deficit/hyperactivity disorder 47, **47**; conduct disorder 48–50; cultural perspectives of 51–55; major depressive disorder 48; support for students with 55–57
migrant children 1, 29–32, 36–37, 39–40, 55
multicultural content integration 7, 71–72, 86–87, 101
multidimensional multicultural education 18–19
multi-tiered culturally responsive system of support (MTCRSS) 19–20, 26, 101–103; and at-risk students 36–40,

55–57, 68–74, 85–90; and implications for practice 24–26; overview of 20–21; primary prevention 21–22, 37–39, 55–56, 68–72, 86–87, 101–102; school climate and 95–98; secondary prevention 22–23, 39–40, 56–57, 72–73, 87–88; tertiary prevention 23–24, 40, 57, 73–74, 88
multi-tiered systems of support (MTSS) 2, 6, 12, *13*, 20, 102; CRE integration with 9–10; theories underpinning 15–17

National School Climate Council (NSCC) 92–93
New Zealand 30, 33, 64

office discipline referrals (ODRs) 5
out-of-home care (OOHC) 65–74, **65**

Palmieri, L. 66, 68–69, 72–73
parents: anxiety disorders and 48; and chronic illness 51; conduct disorder and 49; of ELLs 30; and LGBT+ curricula 85; of LGBT+ students 88; and LGBT+ teachers 81; and low socioeconomic backgrounds 62–63; of migrant children 31–32; MTCRSS and 21, 25, 39, 69–72, 74, 86; and out-of-home care 65–66; parent-educator relationships 50; and perceptions of disability or illness 53, 55; prejudice reduction and 8; and school climate 92, 94, 97; of trans students 90
personalised learning plan (PLP) 46
policies: CRP and 18; implementation science and 15; indigenous students and 33; juvenile justice systems and 74; and LGBT+ students 82–87, 90; out-of-home care and 70; refugee students and 32; RtI and 14; and school climate 98; students with disabilities and 46
Positive Behavioural Interventions and Supports (PBIS) 1–2, 4–6, *4*, 9, 19; MTCRSS and 21–22, 56; and school climate 96; theories underpinning 12–15
poverty 30, 32–33, 62–63, 70–71
pre-correction 5, 25
prejudice reduction 7–8, 101, 103; MTCRSS and *13*, 37, 40, 56, 69, 71
preservice 84–85
professional development: and conduct disorder 50; and ELLs 30; implementation science and 16; and LGBT+ students 82, 84–85, 87; MTCRSS and 21, 37, 69–70; school climate and 92–94, 98

refugee students 1, 29, 32–33, 36–37, 39–40, 55
relationships: counsellor-principal 84; disability and illness and 52; and generalised anxiety disorders 48; MTCRSS and 69–71; out-of-home care and 66–67; parent-educator 50; school climate and 92, 94–95, 98; student 1, 9, 39–40, 75
Response to Intervention (RtI) 1–4, 6, 9, 12, 14–15, 18–21
Richards *see* Gagnon

safety 5, 38, 83, 87–89, 92–93, 95, 97
school climate 1, 92–93, 99, 101–102; dimensions of 93–95; implementation science and 16; LGBT+ students and 80–81, 83, 85–86, 90; and MTCRSS support 95–98; PBIS and 6; *see also* empowering school culture
school culture *see* empowering school culture
second language acquisition 34–36, 38
setting: classroom 1; culturally responsive education and 18; general education 2–3; implementation science and 16; juvenile justice 70; migrant children and 31; school climate 93–95; second language acquisition and 34–35
Skinner, B. F. 13, 34
socioeconomic status (SES) 1, 14, 22, 55; and at-risk students 61–64, 70–73, 75; migrant children and 32
students *see* at-risk students
students of color 101
Sugai, G. 17, 19–20
Swanson, K. 81, 84, 88

teacher 101–102; constructionism learning theory and 18; and ELLs 30; equity pedagogy and 8; and indigenous students 33; knowledge construction and 7–8; and LGBT+ students 81–88; and low socioeconomic backgrounds 63; and major depressive disorder 48; MTCRSS and 21, 24–25; and out-of-home care 66; primary prevention and 22, 55–56, 68–72; and research-based strategies 25–26; RtI and 14–15; and school climate 92–93, 96–97; secondary prevention and 23, 56–57, 73; tertiary prevention and 23, 57, 74; theory of multidimensional multicultural education

and 18–19; universal design for learning and 19
testing 1, 9, 31, 87
theory of action 12, 16–17
theory of change 12, 16–17
trans students 79–80, 87, 89–90
UK 32, 44–45, 50, 53, 62–64, 81
universal design for learning (UDL) 12, 19, 25, 38
US 30–32, 44, 50, 53, 62–64, 81

Zola *see* Groce